A Treasury of
Virginia Tales

Webb Garrison

RUTLEDGE HILL PRESS
Nashville, Tennessee

Published in Nashville, Tennessee, by Rutledge Hill Press, Inc., 211 Seventh Avenue North, Nashville, Tennessee 37219

Typography by Bailey Typography, Inc., Nashville, Tennessee

Library of Congress Cataloging-in-Publication Data

A Treasury of Virginia tales / [edited by] Webb Garrison.
    p.   cm.
   Includes index.
   ISBN 1-55853-097-5
   1. Virginia—History—Anecdotes. I. Garrison, Webb B.
F226.6.T74   1991   90-24434
975.5—dc20   CIP

Printed in the United States of America
3 4 5 6 7 8 — 96 95 94

No Way to Avoid Superlatives!

Delighted at Virginia's loyalty to the Crown, King Charles II of England called it the "Old Dominion." Originally a commonwealth, it is universally famous as the "Mother of Presidents."

Its full story would include tales of the land stretching south to Spanish Florida and west to the Mississippi River. Because so many states were carved from it, Virginia also is the "Mother of States."

Her sons and daughters, by birth and by choice, have had lasting impact upon virtually every sphere of American life. The Old Dominion ranks first in many categories, oldest in others, and strangest in more respects than most of her citizens realize.

Because of space limitations, I have avoided repeating in familiar form stories that are very well known.

In dealing with people and events that are usually part of what is taught in school, I have focused upon little-known and sometimes bizarre aspects. Other tales included here deal with persons and happenings not often remembered even by those fortunate enough to call the Old Dominion their home.

Numerous old letters, proclamations, and other documents are briefly quoted. Except in cases where spelling and language make them hard to understand, the original text has been retained. For the sake of readability, however, short paragraphs are used instead of the page-long paragraphs standard among our forebears.

All persons and events central to these tales are treated in sources available in public or specialized libraries. Since tradition often enhances (and sometimes embellishes) published accounts, oral history has been used freely. Some dialogue is quoted verbatim, but much of it represents what those involved may reasonably be regarded to have said under the circumstances.

Most shrines, museums, tourist centers, and Virginia state agencies I contacted provided quick and useful information, but two agents of the federal government did not. A telephone call to the superintendent of Arlington National Cemetery brought no reply, and a letter to the superintendent of Arlington House apparently went into the trash basket. If you wonder why persons linked with what is now the Robert E. Lee Memorial refused to answer questions, turn to chapter 4.

Preparing this collection of tales—my fourth dealing with southeastern states—brought me a great deal of satisfaction. Here's hoping that as you delve into these tales, you will share my pleasure as your horizons, too, are expanded.

—Webb Garrison
Lake Junaluska, North Carolina
November 1990

Contents

PART ONE

Momentous Deeds in the Old Dominion

In Virginia's waters and on her soil, epoch-making events began taking place more than three hundred years ago when an acting governor planned and executed a raid upon another colony in a successful bid to end piracy on the Atlantic coast.

Armed struggles aside, the Old Dominion was the site of some of the most momentous actions of the Civil War, often overlooked even by native-born Virginians.

Explorer Alexander Spotswood was knighted for his expedition that reached the Susquehanna River.

1

Alexander Spotswood Put an End to Piracy

"Are you game for a good fight, Lieutenant?"

Robert Maynard of the warship *Pearl* bristled and started to rise from his chair.

"Sit down, man, sit down! I meant no harm."

"Perhaps not, Your Excellency, but you know I am an officer of the Royal Navy. I have never shrunk from combat and never will."

Governor Alexander Spotswood nodded understanding, then explained: "If you agree to my undertaking, you will be in no ordinary fight. It is my purpose to put an end to piracy in these waters."

"I thought Virginia's coast was now safe . . ."

"By no means. Near Cape Charles, buccaneers took over the sloop *Betty* not long ago. Once her hold was empty of Madeira wine, they scuttled her. Now they have taken refuge in North Carolina, a colony that has been out of control since it was given its own governor."

"I take it that you plan to launch an invasion of Carolina, a region over which you have no authority?"

Sir Alexander Spotswood remained silent for a moment, then responded soberly: "I have no choice in the matter. These brigands infest Virginia waters. I have it on good authority that they have even beached their vessels on our coast to clear the hulls of barnacles.

"Bath Town, in North Carolina, has become a haven for pirates. The man called Blackbeard has established his vessels in Ocracoke Inlet, and good intelligence has it that he is preparing to erect fortified works."

"I know very little about the New World," countered Maynard, "but I have been told that officials of the Crown make their residence in Bath Town."

"That they do, man! Governor Robert Eden has established himself just across the river from the town. But he will do nothing. Rumor has it that he profits from depredations of the pirates."

"Is there proof that His Majesty's governor sanctions piracy?"

"No proof," admitted the chief executive of Virginia. "But incriminating documents have come into my hands. They indicate that Tobias Knight is aiding and abetting piracy, in return for a good one-third of all the loot that is seized."

"I don't believe I know that name. Who is Knight?"

"He is secretary of the colony and collector of customs. Also a member of the council, recently made chief justice. He can get whatever supplies are needed to fortify Ocracoke Island, perhaps even cannon.

"I have decided to strike by land and by sea before the place becomes too strong to attack. Will you lead vessels of the expedition?"

"I am willing, Sir Alexander. But I doubt very much that London will give permission for warships stationed in Chesapeake Bay to engage in action within waters of a sister colony."

"Of course not! This is a private enterprise, wholly financed by me and employing rented sloops. All I need from you is a handshake guaranteeing your leadership, along with recruitment of your sailors for three weeks of action that will bring them much prize money."

"You propose, then, to treat captured vessels and their contents as prizes?"

"Certainly! And I think you know that the lion's share of prize money goes to the commander."

Robert Maynard nodded understanding and extended his hand. "I am convinced, Your Excellency. Please detail for me your precise plan of action."

Although he was a newcomer to Virginia, the officer who agreed to lead an attack upon the notorious pirate

Blackbeard had heard a great deal about the man who planned the expedition.

Born in Tangier, Morocco, Alexander Spotswood was the son of a physician who attended British troops stationed there. At age seventeen he became an ensign in a foot regiment and fought throughout the War of the Spanish Succession. Wounded in the battle of Blenheim—and by then a lieutenant colonel—his exchange was personally negotiated by the duke of Marlborough. Shortly afterward, perhaps through the influence of Marlborough, he became lieutenant governor of Virginia.

George Hamilton, earl of Orkney, had no intention of going to the colony of which the king had made him governor. In return for half the salary of his subordinate and agent, he relegated management of the New World venture to Spotswood. Although the title was never formally conferred upon him, the physician's son functioned as governor of Virginia.

Spotswood took office on June 23, 1710, and quickly made friends and enemies. His decision to make effective the writ of habeas corpus, previously withheld from the

King George I, who gave the lucrative governorship to the Earl of Orkney, a man who never set foot in Virginia.

province, was cheered everywhere. However, he soon began to regulate the tobacco trade, demanding inspection of all produced for export or offered as security for legal tender. Furious at this edict, wealthy planters started making plans for his removal.

Spotswood led a band of adventurers, servants, and rangers across the Blue Ridge Mountains in 1716. They found a broad, fertile valley which they explored all the way to a river the governor dubbed the Euphrates (now the Shenandoah). To commemorate the expedition and to foster interest in the West, he gave each member of his group a golden horseshoe.

When word of the first exploration of "the great mountains" reached England, King George I rewarded Spotswood with knighthood and sent him a golden horseshoe set with precious stones. That launched the Order of the Golden Horseshoe, America's first fellowship reminiscent of the age of chivalry.

It pained him, Sir Alexander explained to Lieutenant Maynard, that affairs of state made it impossible for him to lead the planned strike against piracy. Already, he had persuaded Capt. Ellis Brand of the warship *Lyme* to head a body of troops that would proceed by land to Bath Town. Maynard's agreement to strike simultaneously by sea meant that the governor's cherished plan could soon be put to the test.

"I have hired two fine sloops," he explained to Maynard. "There are numerous sand bars and reefs in the vicinity of Ocracoke; a warship could not maneuver in those waters. Despite the fact that the vessels you will command are of light draft, you must send a rowboat ahead of them to take soundings. Otherwise, you will find yourself hard aground and an easy target for guns of the pirates."

Pilots familiar with North Carolina waters were put aboard rented sloops that carried fifty-five fighting men. Members of the Virginia council were not informed because Spotswood feared that if lawmakers learned of his plan, they might demand a halt.

Maynard's vessels left Hampton on November 17, 1718,

Ready to split Maynard's skull, Blackbeard was shot by an English seaman.

and worked their way close to "Blackbeard's Hole." Well before sunrise on November 22, he ordered his men to weigh anchors and move toward the pirate ship *Adventure*, known to carry eight cannon.

Momentarily caught on sandbars despite having used rowboats to take soundings, the attacking vessels were raked by fire from Blackbeard's guns. A single blast left more than half of Maynard's men dead or wounded.

Spotswood had foreseen such a development, and he had given detailed advice to Maynard: "If you are hit hard, send below every man who can walk. With weapons at the ready, wait until pirates board your vessel. Then rush up, take them by surprise, and finish them off!"

Following that plan, sailors below decks heard grappling irons from the pirate ship hit their sloop. At a signal, they rushed to the blood-smeared deck and fired their pistols at the astonished pirates.

Robert Maynard personally engaged Blackbeard and exchanged shots. In the melee, the pirate missed, but Maynard's shot hit home. Wounded, the pirate grabbed his cutlass and quickly broke the blade of Maynard's sword near the hilt. As Blackbeard lifted his weapon to split Maynard's skull, a British seaman seized a weapon from the deck and killed the pirate leader on the spot.

The death of their leader and nearly a dozen of his men ended resistance by the pirates. Captives were clapped in irons, and Blackbeard's severed head was hung from the bowsprit of Maynard's vessel. Meanwhile, in Bath Town, Brand and his men seized immense quantities of tobacco, sugar, cotton, and indigo, part of it hidden under hay in a barn belonging to Tobias Knight.

Alexander Spotswood's successful foray into a colony over which he had no authority effectively ended piracy along the Atlantic coast of British America. Before the captured pirates were hanged in Virginia, however, Maynard learned to his consternation that the governor had not revealed his chief motive for taking action.

Continually at odds with members of his own council, the explorer-adventurer who governed Virginia faced probable recall by the Crown. The receiver general of the colony, William Byrd, was then in London bearing a petition to King George. If the monarch acted favorably, the governor's career would be ended.

Only a truly dramatic achievement could offset the barrage of complaints, Spotswood had calculated. Hence the founder of the Order of the Golden Horseshoe put an end to piracy, not so much for the good of the realm, but in a successful bid to remain in office a few more years.

_____

2

Nat Turner Set Out to Liberate Blacks of Southampton County

Hark got a ladder and set it against the chimney [of the Joseph Travis home], on which I ascended, and hoisting a window, entered and came down stairs, unbarred the door, and removed the guns from their places.

It was then observed that I must spill the first blood. On which, armed with a hatchet, and accompanied by Will, I entered my master's chamber: it being, I could not give a death-blow, the hatchet glanced from his head, he sprang from the bed and called his wife: it was his last word.

Will laid him dead, with a blow of his axe, and Mrs. Travis shared the same fate, as she lay in bed.

The murder of this family, five in number, was the work of a moment, not one of them awoke: there was a little infant sleeping in a cradle, that was forgotten, until we had left the house and gone some distance, when Henry and Will returned and killed it; we got here, four guns that would shoot, and several old muskets, with a pound or two of powder.

T. R. Gray of Jerusalem, Virginia, appointed to defend the leader of an insurrection, used his relationship with the defendant to record his personal account of two bloody days. As published in Baltimore, *The Confessions of Nat Turner* ran to twenty-two pages.

Even the *Richmond Enquirer*, in whose pages portions were reprinted on November 25, 1831, noted that "the language is far superior to what Nat Turner could have employed." This factor, wrote the editors, "is calculated to cast some shade of doubt over the authenticity of the narrative." Yet the booklet is the only firsthand source of insight into the mind and actions of the leader of the nation's last great slave uprising.

Believed to have been born late in 1800 on the South-ampton County plantation of Benjamin Turner, Nat was later known by the surname of the planter. Before age thirty, he had been passed from one owner to another at frequent in-tervals: Samuel Turner, Thomas Moore, and Putnam Moore who hired him to Joseph Travis.

Nancy, mother of the strange little boy, was fiercely pro-tective. When other slaves suggested that he might be "tetched in the head" or mentally unstable, Nancy insisted that Nat "sure ain't touched a bit; he's inspired by the Lord."

Taught by Nancy to see himself as a divinely ordained prophet, Nat began to preach very early in life. His fiery pro-nouncements helped elevate him to a leadership role among slaves of adjoining plantations.

Eventually, he began scanning the sky in search of signs. Once messages began coming to him from the heavens, he learned to find other signs in the shapes and movements of leaves. Then he started hearing voices from nowhere, speak-ing words that only he heard. At age twenty-one he had a heavenly vision of such force that he was led to baptize a white man.

On February 12, 1831, Nat Turner received the most powerful sign he had yet encountered. Most people called it an eclipse of the sun, but he knew it was a message from God that called him to deliver the slaves of Southampton County from their masters.

Unstable though he was, the black prophet was far from stupid. Realizing he had few friends whom he could trust, he set July 4 as the day on which to launch his war of libera-tion but spoke of his plan only in guarded hints. Con-sequently, July 4 came and went without incident.

Five weeks later, much of Southampton County was covered all day with a peculiar haze. Old timers shook their heads in bewilderment and said they had never seen any-thing quite like it; the sun seemed to be bluish green for hour after hour. However, Nat Turner knew the awesome sign in the heavens was meant for him: Almighty God was commanding him to get about his mission.

Cautiously, he sounded out two men he thought he could trust. Hark listened attentively, nodded often, and said it

Nat Turner (center) exhorts early recruits.

was time to act. Henry was more cautious, but he became enthusiastic as he considered the prospect of ridding the region of white men so former slaves could be masters of land, cattle, and houses. Then Henry and Hark needed only a few hours to recruit Nelson, Sam, Jack, and Will.

At midafternoon on August 21, Nat Turner and his six followers gathered at Cabin Pond. After killing and cooking a stolen pig, they drank brandy and made plans. About two hours after midnight, they proceeded to the Travis homestead. It was there, according to Nat, that "Hark got a ladder" and the insurgents embarked upon wholesale slaughter.

Viewed in retrospect, there was no pattern to their selection of victims. They murdered whatever whites they happened to find.

Soon joined by other recruits, the band grew to perhaps fifty, then dwindled rapidly as resistance mounted. By the time it numbered no more than twenty, it was an easy task for the militia to kill Will, disperse the band, and drive Nat into hiding.

Before that armed confrontation took place, Nat and his followers had murdered fifty-five whites, mostly entire families made up largely of women and children. Mrs. Levi Williams and her ten boys and girls were the largest family group slaughtered.

Nat fled when his followers failed to withstand attack. Drinking from creeks and eating berries and roots, he eluded capture for more than two months. About noon on October 30, young Benjamin Phipps discovered him while walking in the fields about a mile and one-half from the Travis home, where the first murders were committed. When he noticed strange movements in branches piled over what appeared to be a cave, he turned aside for a closer look. Turner saw him approaching, stood up, threw out his only weapon—a rusty sword—and surrendered.

Phipps held Turner overnight, then took him to Jerusalem where he turned him over to authorities. Although he protested that he had done nothing heroic, he accepted several rewards that yielded about twelve hundred dollars.

In addition to Turner, forty-four slaves and five free blacks were put on trial as co-conspirators. Only four were juveniles, listed in trial records as "boys." Ten were convicted and were transported while seventeen, including Turner, went to the gallows.

Few recorded uprisings have been crushed so quickly and completely. During the spree of murders and its aftermath, an estimated eighty blacks not brought to trial were killed by enraged whites. Yet the approximate two to one ratio of black to white deaths was the least significant result of the uprising led by a zealot.

By coincidence, William Lloyd Garrison issued the first edition of his antislavery newspaper, *The Liberator*, on January 1, 1831, just before the rebellion. In it he labeled all owners of slaves as "not within the pale of Christianity, of Republicanism, of humanity." He condemned the U.S. Constitution as "a league with death and a covenant with Hell." Despite accusations of those whom he attacked, Garrison did not directly encourage slaves to plan and execute the murders of their masters, but his newspaper reported every such killing known to the editor. Illiterate, Nat Turner probably never heard of William Lloyd Garrison's newspaper. Yet the coincidence in timing between its appearance and the launching of the insurrection gave ammunition to foes of abolition.

Angry lawmakers of Georgia passed a bill that offered five thousand dollars for the arrest and conviction of William Lloyd Garrison. In South Carolina, the statewide Vigilance Association offered to pay one thousand dollars to any person showing that he had captured a distributor of *The Liberator* "or any other seditious publications." Throughout the South, legislators enacted new and sterner measures designed to prevent a repetition of "the Virginia massacre."

Until it took place, southern societies formed to foster emancipation had been gaining in strength. Suddenly, members of such groups found themselves under such social pressure that they gave up.

Without having the slightest understanding of his long-range effect, the man who considered himself a divinely appointed liberator greatly increased polarization between already divided sections of the United States. More than any other black who used force in an attempt to overthrow slavery, Nat Turner helped to create a climate in which more and more people accepted the coming of civil war as inevitable.

Nat Turner (left) carried only a sword at the time of his capture [SCRIBNER'S POPULAR HISTORY].

3

Virginia Coast Was Site of First Step toward Emancipation of Slaves

"Where was the death knell of slavery first sounded? Not in the United States Senate, not in the House of Representatives, and not in the White House! Where, then you ask? At the southeastern tip of Virginia, my friends!

"You laugh, and doubt my word. But it is true. I know; I was there!"

Repeated frequently with minor variations, that message was delivered by James M. Ashley at Montana political rallies. Once listeners stopped smiling at one another and shaking their heads, the ex-governor of the territory (a Republican who earlier had been a prominent Democrat) made an even more startling announcement.

"'Who sounded the tocsin?' you ask. Not a valiant Republican abolitionist. Not a crusading newspaper editor. Not a pulpit giant. Simply a doggedly stubborn military man who was Abe Lincoln's first brigadier general, and a Democrat, to boot!"

At the outset of the Civil War, the man who was then a congressman from Ohio sent a lengthy and rambling dispatch to the *Toledo Blade*. Here greatly condensed, the newspaper report dealt with slaves. During the evening of May 23, 1861, three runaways had managed to reach Fort Monroe, named for the Virginia-born president, at the southeastern tip of the state.

Maj. Gen. Benjamin Butler, who had assumed command of the Federal installation the previous day, was notified that a trio of "field hands belonging to Col. Charles K. Mallory, now heading secession forces in the district," had surrendered to the picket guard.

Benjamin F. Butler, first Maj. Gen. named by Lincoln, owed his high post to being an influential Democrat [MATHEW BRADY STUDIO, LIBRARY OF CONGRESS].

Eight days earlier the military leader had gone to the White House to receive his commission from President Lincoln. According to Ashley, Butler gave his personal attention to the slaves as soon as he learned of their presence. When questioned, they said they were about to be shipped to Carolina to aid secession forces there.

"As these men were very serviceable, and I had great need of labor in my quartermaster's department, I determined to avail myself of them," Butler reported to Gen. Winfield Scott. To avoid being charged with violating the Fugitive Slave Law, the man who had been on Virginia soil for less than forty-eight hours sent a receipt to Colonel Mallory. That document was similar to other notices sent to private citizens whose property was seized "for the exigencies of the [military] service."

"Negroes in this neighborhood," Butler told his commanding general, "are now being employed in the erection of batteries and other works by the rebels."

He then framed a question that was the heart of his detailed dispatch: "Should rebels be allowed the use of this property against the United States, and we not be allowed its use in aid of the United States?"

The question was profound in 1861, and General Scott requested a formal ruling from the secretary of war, Simon Cameron.

Well before Cameron gave his approval to Butler's decision to put the runaways to work "in the service to which they may be best adapted," the man in command of Fort Monroe was notified that a messenger was approaching under a flag of truce. Major Cary of the Virginia militia, ushered into the presence of General Butler, introduced himself as an attorney, presented his military credentials, and demanded that Mallory's "happy and contented slaves" be turned over to him at once, as required by federal law.

According to James M. Ashley, Butler offered to relinquish the fugitives "if their master would come to the fort and take the oath of allegiance to the Constitution of the United States."

Bristling, the Confederate messenger dismissed that proposal as preposterous. He then argued that the slaves were the property of a Virginian who was no longer a citizen of the United States.

"You hold that Negro slaves are property and that Virginia is no longer a part of the United States?"

"I do, sir," responded Cary.

"You are a lawyer, sir," Butler said. "I want to know if you claim that the Fugitive Slave Act of the United States is binding in a foreign nation; and if a foreign nation uses this kind of property to destroy the lives and property of citizens of the United States, if that species of property ought not to be regarded as contraband?"

According to Ashley, "This was too much for the colonel and he knocked under and withdrew."

Northern newspapers quickly picked up the colorful story, emphasizing the manner in which Butler made an on-the-spot decision to label runaway slaves as "contraband of war." Soon the impromptu and unofficial term became standard. Along every military front, Union officers received blacks as contrabands, then refused to return them to their owners and put them to work as blacksmiths, laborers, cooks, and hostlers.

Continuing his account for the *Toledo Blade*, the Ohio congressman offered readers his own opinion: "This was but the beginning at Fort Monroe, and is but the beginning of a question which this Administration must meet and determine, viz., 'What shall be done with the slaves who refuse to fight against the Government of the United States and escape from the traitors and come into our camps?'

"If the Administration meets this question as it ought, well; if not, it will prove its overthrow.

"It is a question of more magnitude and importance than the rebellion itself; and woe to the public man or the party who proves false to the demands of humanity and justice."

At the time Ashley submitted his views to the public following Butler's decision to ignore the Fugitive Slave Law under which owners could reclaim runaway slaves anywhere in the United States, Abraham Lincoln favored adherence to the law. Like the great majority of men whom he called to fight, the president was concerned with preservation of the Union, not with the abolition of slavery.

Had General Butler consulted Lincoln, he would have

A contraband settlement at an unidentified location [MATHEW BRADY STUDIO, LIBRARY OF CONGRESS].

been informed that Virginia and other states were "in a state of rebellion" but were not regarded as foreign nations. Hence the laws of the United States were, in theory, just as applicable to Virginia as to Maine, and Butler's refusal to deliver slaves to their owner was an open-and-shut violation of federal law. As a veteran criminal lawyer, Butler knew that as well as did Lincoln.

Yet by applying the military label of "contraband" to humans who belonged to secessionists, Butler created a loophole whose magnitude was far greater than he imagined. Before the end of July, the installation he commanded was crowded with one thousand contrabands. They also swarmed into bases as widely separated as Port Royal, South Carolina, and Fort Warren, Massachusetts. So many followed Sherman's army on the March to the Sea that the Ohio-born general did all he could to get rid of them.

Prodded into action by events in Virginia, legislators in the Federal capital pondered the question of what to do with slaves. In August 1861, Congress passed the hotly contested Confiscation Act. Under its terms, any fugitive slave who had been employed in work calculated to advance the cause of the Confederacy was termed "a prize of war" who should be set free.

"Morning Mustering of the Contraband at Fortress Monroe" [LESLIE'S ILLUSTRATED, NOVEMBER 2, 1861].

Neither the president nor Congress was willing to come to terms with the question of emancipation; confiscation was as far as they would go. Even Lincoln's Emancipation Proclamation did not pretend to free slaves whose masters were residing in Union-held territory and who were loyal to the Union.

Many contrabands were used by Federal military leaders as laborers, and some were leased to Unionist planters. Great numbers were crowded into makeshift camps, in which mortality rates were sometimes nearly as bad as all but the worst military prisons.

Still the contrabands came, in ever-growing numbers. Eventually recognized as a new pool of manpower for the military, blacks were for the first time offered blue uniforms when slaves in rebel territory were proclaimed to be free.

Precisely what sort of man made the first concrete step toward breaking the fetters of slavery? Now regarded as one of the least effective of Abraham Lincoln's "political generals," Butler protested when ordered to Fort Monroe. His new assignment was more than a demotion; it was a flagrant insult. Relieved of command in all-important Maryland and told to go to a remote spot in Virginia, he demanded (without avail) to see both Gen. Winfield Scott and President Abraham Lincoln.

Was his defiance of federal law within hours after reaching Fort Monroe a nose-thumbing exercise directed at his superiors in Washington, or was it simply a seat-of-the-trousers decision in a difficult situation? No one really knows what caused him to take the first fumbling step toward freedom for all Americans.

This much is certain, however: Ben Butler never wavered after having made up his mind. The man who gave new meaning to the concept of contraband of war was a Massachusetts delegate to the Democratic convention of 1860. There he not only took the floor to offer resolutions from "a minority of one," he also voted to nominate Jefferson Davis of Mississippi for the U.S. presidency, not once but on fifty-seven consecutive ballots.

4

"Let Lee's Mansion Be First to Fall"

"Gentlemen, I know you are wondering why I have called you here."

"Not really," responded Samuel P. Heintzelman, a brigadier general of U.S. Volunteers who was serving as acting inspector general of the Department of Washington. "We've been sitting on our hands for more than a month since the secessionists fired on Sumter. Some of us old-time West Pointers have been wondering when we'd get a chance to strike our own first blow. This is it, I presume?"

"I suppose you could say so, in a fashion," nodded his immediate superior, white-maned Gen. Joseph K. F. Mansfield. "But we must not use such language, General. Let it be clearly understood that we have come together to make plans for the defense of Washington and the security of the president, my own primary responsibilities."

Mansfield paused to permit his meaning to sink into the minds of his aides.

"As an engineer," he continued, "as soon as I took command of this department, I realized that the capital—and the president—cannot be secure until we have Arlington Heights in our hands.

"All of you know the region well?" he inquired, clucking with satisfaction as every head nodded assent. "This region is barely two miles from executive offices and other government buildings. Some of the best new artillery—hopefully not yet in the hands of secessionists—will throw shells a good four miles. We must act speedily, before our enemies have a chance to bring guns to bear upon this city.

"Once we have staved off disaster by seizing the region, it

Mrs. Robert E. Lee, the former Mary Custis.

will be necessary to throw up defensive earthworks there, an undertaking of such magnitude that it must be launched as soon as possible."

"Excuse me, General," interrupted Gen. C. W. Sandford of the New York Militia. "I know I'm here because my troops are in the city and are itching to fight. But if I understand you correctly, sir, you are talking about invasion of Virginia."

"Not at all," snapped Mansfield. "You know, and I know, and citizens at large know that Mr. Lincoln made a solemn promise to the Virginians who came here to talk peace, unaware that supply ships were already on the way to Fort Sumter. He gave them his word that the soil they hold so sacred will never be invaded."

"Then why waste time talking of throwing up earthworks on Arlington Heights?"

"Because the operation that you and your colleagues are to undertake is a *defensive* exercise, pure and simple. To be sure, it will be executed upon Virginia soil. But—"

"Our commanding general is a native of the Old Dominion," interrupted an aide to Gen. Winfield Scott. "Between us, that is the reason he is not presiding over our meeting. Under extreme pressure from President Lincoln, he has concluded that the term *invasion* must be interpreted to mean a hostile incursion not undertaken for defensive purposes. Since we now propose to include Arlington Heights within the defensive perimeter of this city, seizure of the place will not constitute an invasion in the true sense of that term."

Col. Charles P. Stone of Greenfield, Massachusetts, included in the conference because he was personally charged with preserving the safety of the nation's capital, squirmed restlessly and started to speak. Then he changed his mind. Clearly, the decision to move into Virginia had been made in the White House, regardless of explanations offered by senior officers. That being the case, it would be futile to protest. Stone swallowed his half-formed protest and said nothing.

"What about the town of Alexandria? I believe it holds a considerable number of militia units?" inquired Heintzelman.

"Our troops must by-pass the town. It is not essential to our defensive plans."

"My men are itching to move into action," responded the 1826 graduate of West Point, a descendant of German immigrants. "When do we start across the Potomac?"

"Only when we receive word from the very highest quarters," responded Mansfield. "Virginians will vote on secession in just a few days. It would be appropriate to wait until citizens have endorsed the proclamation issued by their governor on the heels of Fort Sumter."

"If Arlington and only Arlington is our goal," mused Sandford, "I believe we will be charged with taking possession of the estate of Robert E. Lee."

"Right," nodded the presiding officer. "Let Lee's mansion be first to fall! But, mind you, gentlemen, not a word about our plans to anyone except your own key subordinates, and tell them as little as possible. Just make sure that their units are ready to move at an hour's notice."

Various streams of oral tradition preserve fragments of the conference over which Mansfield presided. No one present was willing to admit, then or ever, that it actually was a council of war called to make plans for invasion of the South.

Assignments made up on the afternoon of May 23, 1861, were revised and amplified within hours. As a result, when ten thousand Federal troops began moving out of the capital in bright moonlight, several units were instructed to capture and if necessary reduce Alexandria, Virginia.

Newspaper editors rejoiced when they discovered that rumors, floating about for two or three weeks, were soon to be confirmed. It was appropriate, some of them told their readers, that Virginia, "more than any other state responsible for the great rebellion," should be the first to feel the tread of marching columns of Union soldiers. Besides, they pointed out, "our commanders can move one-fourth of our forces into Virginia in one-fourth of the time it will take secessionists to put their own into that region."

Mrs. Robert E. Lee had inherited Arlington from her father, grandson of Martha Washington. An increasingly limited near-invalid, she was urged by letters from her husband to leave posthaste. However, she reported to him that she was in correspondence with Gen. Winfield Scott and Gen. Irvin McDowell. Happily, McDowell had promised to protect Arlington, so she felt no fear.

About May 14, she learned of the Federal plans. Frightened for the first time, Mrs. Lee left so hurriedly that many Washington relics and other treasures were left behind. Only the silver was safe, having been shipped to Lexington earlier, where it was buried.

Just ten days after the wife of the Confederate commander of Virginia forces fled from the mansion in which she had been born and reared, Federal troops seized it and the surrounding region. General Sandford reported to General Scott on May 26 that he had completed "examination of the roads and woods in the vicinity of Arlington." Already, he wrote, he was building a road that would cut through the woods behind Arlington House.

While the new road was still under construction, Gen. Irvin McDowell selected Arlington House as his headquarters. He found that the mansion, built in 1802, still held many memorabilia, despite forty-eight hours of looting. In the entry there were portraits of Revolutionary leaders painted by George Washington Custis, and three deer heads from animals killed by George Washington adorned the dining room. A splendid likeness of the duke of Wellington was faced by a full-length oil painting of Robert E. Lee's Revolutionary War hero father, "Lighthorse Harry" Lee.

Distressed that many pieces of furniture and numerous small objects had already been taken by soldiers, McDowell decided to safeguard the artifacts that were left and sent them across the Potomac, where they were placed on exhibit at the patent office. *Captured at Arlington* proclaimed the placard above a punch bowl, wash stand, mirror, part of a set of china given by Lafayette to George Washington, a few of Washington's tent poles and pins, and a pair of breeches and waistcoat once worn by the Father of His Country.

After the Civil War ended, Mrs. Abraham Lincoln wrote President Andrew Johnson, asking that the artifacts be returned. He appeared ready to comply with her request, but before he could act, Gen. John A. Logan persuaded a congressional committee to take action. Following secret hearings, the committee decided that any move "to deliver [the Washington relics] to the rebel General Robert E. Lee is an insult to the loyal people of the United States."

Meanwhile, Congress had taken drastic steps that directly involved the estate belonging to Lee's wife. In June 1862 a law was enacted that imposed a direct tax upon real estate "in the insurrectionary districts." Commissioners were selected, then given power to assess and collect taxes. Under the law, default by an owner meant that property could be sold for taxes.

Once they assumed their duties, the commissioners decided not to accept payment of taxes by any person other than the owner in person. This meant that men who were far from home wearing Confederate gray would be helpless to meet the demands of federal agents.

Arlington—not simply the mansion, but also the surrounding estate that included three hundred acres of splendid woodlands—was assessed at just under one hundred dollars. Philip R. Fendall, a cousin of the Custis family, was late in tendering the taxes due. Hence he brought along an

Arlington, with invaders posed on the steps [Photographic History of the Civil War].

additional 50 percent with which to pay a penalty. Because he was not the legal owner, the commissioners refused to accept payment.

Therefore, the estate was sold in January 1864 for delinquent taxes, a transaction that involved a bookkeeping transfer of $26,680 from one federal account to another. Eight months later, a tax-sale title was issued to the United States of America.

Robert E. Lee confided to a friend that the sale of furniture, animals, and trees "should have been sufficient to more than meet the taxes." He thought, correctly, that federal officials believed the estate belonged to him rather than to his wife. Before the new title was issued, they had agreed that Arlington would be used as a cemetery for Union soldiers.

When presidents of the United States failed to restore Arlington to its owner, Mrs. Lee's oldest son and heir, George, eventually retained attorneys and launched a long-drawn-suit aimed at regaining the family tract. In 1882 the U.S. Supreme Court ruled in favor of the plaintiff, but by that time tens of thousands of graves covered much of the estate. Regretfully, Lee accepted $150,000 from Congress for one of Virginia's most valuable plantations.

Arlington House, about which the life of the estate revolved, became the first federally owned historic home. Some of the Washington artifacts and some pieces of furniture—also the property of the United States of America—were eventually returned.

Open to visitors free of charge every day of the year except New Year's Day and Christmas, Arlington House is now administered by the National Park Service. Few who visit the mansion and Arlington National Cemetery learn that it was all taken from Martha Washington's descendant for nonpayment of $92.07 in delinquent taxes, which the owner had tried to pay and the government had refused to accept.

PART TWO

Virginia Women Are Truly Special!

Some Virginia women were involved in remarkable first achievements and events. From colonial times to the twentieth century, they have made contributions that men have never successfully surpassed.

Ætatis suæ 21. Aº 1616.

Matoaks als Rebecka daughter to the mighty Prince
Powhatan Emperour of Attanoughkomouck als virginia
converted and baptized in the Christian faith, and
Wife to the worth.^{ll} Mr Tho: Rolff.

This 1616 portrait of Pocahontas is held by the National Gallery of Art.

5

America's First Celebrity Was a Woman

At first glance, the woman in a portrait owned by the National Gallery of Art in Washington, D.C., looks as though she might be an English queen. At second glance, she appears to be a near double of the Virgin Queen, Elizabeth I.

A closer look reveals that the unknown artist was careful to identify his subject. According to his script, she is:

> Matoaks als Rebecka daughter to the mighty Prince Powhatan Emperour of Attanoughkomouch als Virginia converted and baptized in the Christian faith, and Wife to Mr. Tho: Rolff

Here *als* is the artist's abbreviation for "otherwise known as."

How did the portrait of Powhatan's daughter—appearing not at all like a native American—come to be included in holdings of the National Gallery of Art?

It is there because it depicts the first American to become a lionized celebrity, also the first American convert to Christianity, the first American to have a formal church wedding, and the first woman to play a significant role in the establishment of a royal British colony overseas.

Sir Thomas Dale, governor of the New World venture launched by the Virginia Company, was keenly aware that investors had received no return on their money. The original adventurers who had gone to Jamestown in a square-rigged vessel that was smaller than the *Mayflower* had expected to return to England with gold and rubies, but that was not to be.

Had the term *development company* been in vogue then, it would have been attached to the band of those who put money into the venture. Realizing that investors would not gain sudden wealth from Virginia, the officials of the company hoped to bolster its image sufficiently to keep its stock from becoming worthless.

In a move calculated to create new interest in the overseas project, Dale brought to London a colorful native American. He hoped that she would attract wide attention, but he never imagined that she would become one of the most celebrated persons of the day.

Captain John Smith is the sole authority for stories about the first exploit of the girl Matoaka, otherwise known as Pocahontas ("playful one"). Probably the oldest daughter of the chieftain Powhatan, she appeared to the English adventurer to be a "child of tenne years old" when he first saw her.

At the time, Smith was in no condition to pay much attention to a small girl, not even the daughter of a chieftain. Having been captured by Powhatan, he had been thrust into a "long house," or arbor, hastily improvised from boughs. Wearing eagle feathers and raccoon skins, Powhatan presided over the American Indian equivalent of a trial involving a capital offense.

An estimated two hundred warriors stood in rows, their women behind them with down-covered heads above red-painted necks. Smith was brought water with which to wash his hands; then all feasted. When the food was gone, the solemn council of native Americans sentenced the captive to die.

Two large stones were rolled before Powhatan, who gave a signal for the warriors to drag Smith before him. Arms pinioned, the Englishman was forced to place his head upon the stones, then muscular warriors raised their war clubs to bash out his brains.

Suddenly "the king's dearest daughter sprang from her father's side," the ancient narrative reads. She raced to the spot of execution, threw herself upon the prisoner, and laid her own head above his.

That dramatic gesture meant that the warriors would either have to pull the chieftain's daughter away, bash out her

Pocahontas saves the life of John Smith [THEODOR DE BRY ENGRAVING].

brains while crushing the head of the condemned man, or turn him loose.

Since John Smith later wrote *A True Relation of Virginia Since the First Planting of the Colony* (1608) and *The Generall Historie of Virginia* (1624), the Indians obviously spared his life. Though not wholly consistent, both volumes devote space to Pocahontas and her exploits.

Soon the girl came to Jamestown, where she persuaded boys to "go forth with her into the market place" to see who could turn the fastest handsprings. She trusted the palefaces so fully that she hardly knew what was happening when Capt. Samuel Argall of the ship *Treasurer* found her among the Potomacs and seized her as a hostage. His 1613 capture of "the Indian princess," then believed to be perhaps sixteen or eighteen years old, was designed to prevent her tribesmen from killing English prisoners.

Brought back to Jamestown, Pocahontas seems for the first time to have attracted the attention of the colony's head. Thomas Dale, who said he was touched by her intelligence and gentleness, set out to have her "carefully instructed in Christian Religion."

One of the persons involved in carrying out Dale's plan was planter John Rolfe, locally renowned for having introduced mild West Indian tobacco into the colony to give Virginia her first product for export. A widower of less than a year, Rolfe became interested in more than the salvation of the girl's soul. Soon he wrote a letter of about 1,700 words in which he asked the governor's permission to wed the Indian princess. By the time he received an affirmative reply to a match that Dale saw as a step toward better relations with all Indians, Pocahontas had been baptized in the tiny Jamestown church. She took the name Rebecca and was told that she would always have a special place in memory because she was the first American convert.

In spite of having taken a biblical name when she stood at a tiny font "hollowed out like a canoe," there is no record that she was widely known as Rebecca. All accounts of her wedding refer to her as Pocahontas.

For Jamestown, the ceremony represented about as grand a celebration as the Virginia colony was capable of producing. Volunteers trimmed the church with wild flowers, holly, and other evergreens. Although simply dressed "in a tunic of white muslin from the looms of Dacca," the radiant bride wore a flowing veil and an embroidered robe that was a gift from the governor.

An account written late in the nineteenth century drips with sentiment:

> A gaudy fillet encircled her head, and held the plumage of birds of gorgeous colors, while her wrists and ankles were adorned with the simple jewelry of the native workshops.
>
> When the ceremony was ended, the eucharist was administered, with bread from the wheat-fields around Jamestown and wine from the grapes of the adjacent forest. Her brothers and sisters and forest maidens were present; also the governor and council, and five Englishwomen—all that were in the colony.

Pocahontas was persuaded to visit the ship of Captain Argall in April 1613 [THEODOR DE BRY ENGRAVING].

Three years after the dramatic 1613 wedding ceremony, Governor Dale, who may have decided upon the scheme much earlier, sent the American princess and her husband to London. If anyone could revive the sagging fortunes of the Virginia Company, surely she could!

Governor Dale's secretary believed that John Rolfe's marriage to "one of rude education, manner barbarous and cursed generation" could only have been "for the good and honour of the Plantation." Whether that was the case or not, her husband soon found himself at the bottom of the pecking order. In London, his wife was hailed as the "Barbarian Princess," but the king thought Rolfe was guilty of a crime because he—a commoner—dared to go to bed with a member of royalty.

Ostensibly brought as a guest of the queen of England, Pocahontas was escorted to the court of both the queen and the king, who maintained separate palaces. Escorted to the

Globe Theatre and to Blackfriars by Lady De La Warr, she became a major celebrity and was said frequently to receive special invitations to play cards with the queen and the ladies of her court. Even the Reverend Dr. King, bishop of London, unbent enough to give a special gala in her honor.

Soon crowds began to gather any time it was rumored that she would be seen in the streets. Artists competed with one another for the privilege of painting her portrait, and street vendors hawked her likeness throughout London and surrounding cities.

Measured by today's standards, the first public relations campaign with an American base was a huge success. It had such impact that King James I decided not to renew the charter of the privately operated Virginia Company. Instead, he made Virginia a royal colony, the first in a series that eventually caused his countrymen to boast that "the sun never sets upon the British Empire."

Though she seemed to thrive upon adulation, Pocahontas fretted that her husband received none. One by one, half of the Indians who had come with her as attendants died of maladies unknown in the New World. So after a year as a sought-after celebrity, she decided to return to Virginia.

Before her ship could sail, she was stricken with one of the plagues of the white man: smallpox. Pocahontas battled the deadly disease only briefly and at her death was buried in an unmarked grave inside the chancel of the church at Gravesend, England.

John Rolfe returned to Virginia. There the widower of a princess became a victim of the 1622 Indian uprising now known as the Great Massacre.

6

Captain Sally Healed More Than One Thousand Wounded Men

"President Davis will see you now, but you must be brief."

"Thank you. With a waiting room full of military men, he is kind to take time to hear a woman's petition. Yet I think he will find it to be urgent."

Opening a door, an aide to Jefferson Davis, president of the Confederate States of America, announced: "Sir, this is Miss Sally Louisa Tompkins, of the Robertson Hospital. Mr. James Mason, who does not have an appointment, is also here and wishes to see you as soon as possible."

"Tell Mason that I will make time for him immediately," the chief executive responded. Turning to his visitor, he shook hands and pointed her to a seat.

"I know more about you than you may think," began the former U.S. secretary of war. "You have been residing here for a number of years, but I believe you grew up in Mathews County."

"Yes, sir, I spent my early years in Poplar Grove, Virginia, a delightful hamlet, where my father had extensive holdings. My mother and I thought it best to remove to Richmond soon after his death. But my business here is not personal. It concerns your recent order closing the private hospitals of the city."

Glancing at his memorandum, the president nodded understanding. "You are nursing some of our sick and wounded in the home turned over to you by Judge Robertson, I believe. What experience did you have prior to establishing the hospital?"

"Very little," Miss Tompkins admitted. "Since my father was wealthy, I devoted much of my time to aiding the sick and the destitute of Poplar Grove. But there were not many of them, and none were suffering from anything like battlefield wounds.

"When our brave soldiers began pouring into the city six weeks ago after the battle at Manassas Junction, there were too many for the hospitals of the city. A good friend of mine opened her home as a hospital, and that gave me the idea of doing the same, only I wanted a much bigger residence. It took less than a day to find that Judge John Robertson was willing to give me the use of a splendid house belonging to him and temporarily unoccupied."

"So it was easy to locate suitable quarters," mused the president. "There were sick and wounded men aplenty. But how did you go about securing beds and bandages?"

"When my father's estate was settled, I received an ample inheritance. I used my own money to equip the Robertson Hospital. There was plenty left over for food and other essentials. It was not necessary to employ helpers. The brave and gentle women of this city were eager to serve as volunteers."

"A noble enterprise, indeed, young woman. But we are now a nation at war. I am closing all civilian institutions, because military officers can operate hospitals more efficiently."

"How do you measure efficiency, Mr. President?" Sally Tompkins demanded. "Here . . . I have kept a careful list. Robertson Hospital has been in operation, every bed filled, since the second of August. During four full weeks, we have lost only one man, who arrived with his right arm dangling, poor fellow, and his shoulder and thigh riddled with bullet holes."

"That is splendid," Davis admitted. "But I learned years ago that raw mortality figures mean very little. How many of our soldiers have you actually looked after during this period?"

"I have a list of names, ranks, and regiments. I brought it for you to see," responded the Virginia woman. "Look at the bottom. It shows that our Robertson Hospital has cared for

Instead of a weapon, Captain Sally Tompkins wore a nurse's pouch at her waist [VIRGINIA STATE LIBRARY].

forty-one men. A few have been discharged, but most are still there."

"You plead a splendid case, young woman. I wish I could dare to hope that all of our military hospitals would match that record. In spite of the fact that I know they cannot, my orders have already been issued. I cannot countermand them. Thank you for what you have done for our Second American Revolution . . . and may God bless you."

Rising to indicate that the interview was over, Jefferson Davis extended his hand to his visitor. Tradition says that at this point, Sally Louisa began to sob silently, making no move to get up from her chair.

Opening the door, an aide announced briskly, "Mr. Mason has asked me to tell you that his business is urgent, sir, and he can wait only a few minutes more."

"Bring him in," directed the president.

"You must forgive this young woman, Mr. Mason. She will

regain her composure very shortly, I am sure. She is distraught that I have been forced to close the hospital she operates, along with all the rest run by civilians."

"Yes, I know the matter," nodded the man who in March 1861 had resigned the chairmanship of the U.S. Senate Committee on Foreign Affairs. Having accepted appointment as the Confederate States of America emissary to Great Britain, he had found his proposed voyage threatened by the Federal blockade of southern ports.

"I think I have a solution to my transportation problem," James Mason began. "But before exercising it, I believe I should have your approval. I confess that I am disappointed in having found it impossible to board a Confederate vessel headed straight for London.

"Mr. Slidell has received sure intelligence that the British mail-packet *Trent* will be leaving England soon on its regular run. He has proposed that the two of us book passage on this vessel for the return voyage, enabling us to pass through the Federal blockade.

"If your own faithful horse goes lame," he continued with enthusiasm, "the best thing you can do is to borrow a horse from a friend!"

"You have my approval," responded Jefferson Davis soberly. "I am sorry to have detained you. This young woman"—he pointed to a now-composed Sally Tompkins—"made an appointment two days ago, and I was honor bound to see her. Godspeed, sir, as you 'ride a borrowed horse' on your all-important mission."

Sally Tompkins rose and started to follow Mason from the room.

"Wait a moment, Miss Tompkins," directed Jefferson Davis. "Mr. Mason has given me an idea. How would you like to be an officer in our cavalry, in order to ride a horse of your own?"

"I don't understand, sir."

"It has occurred to me that if I give you a commission as an officer, perhaps as a captain—yes, surely a captain, no less and no more—that will place a military officer in charge of the Robertson Hospital. How would you like that?"

Having conceived a plan by which to circumvent his own

C.S.A. President Jefferson Davis made Tompkins an officer in order to permit her hospital to remain in operation.

order, President Davis acted decisively. On September 9, 1861, he signed the commission by which an idealistic young woman became Captain Tompkins of the Confederate cavalry.

"Captain Sally," as she was known for the rest of her life, regularly drew her salary but returned all of it to the government.

Robertson Hospital remained in operation until June 1865. Because the institution had gained a wide reputation, surgeons preferred to send badly wounded men to it, if possible. In spite of caring for a disproportionate number of soldiers whose condition was critical upon arrival, Captain Sally and her staff recorded only 73 deaths from 1,333 admissions. No other Civil War hospital, North or South, had a comparable record.

Confederate veterans, of all ranks and from several states, showered their "angel of mercy" with postwar offers of marriage. She turned down all of them to devote her time, energy, and financial resources to the work of the Episcopal church.

Financial reverses during Reconstruction years left the one-time philanthropist impoverished. Consequently, she took up residence in Richmond's Home for Confederate Women. Never having worn a uniform, at her death in July 1916, the only woman officer of the C.S.A. was buried with full military honors.

7

Teenager Belle Boyd Gained International Renown as a Courier and Spy

"How I wish that I were a man! Nothing would have given me so much pleasure as to have entered the ranks of Company D along with my father! Since that was impossible, I will offer my services as a courier—a female Paul Revere—in our glorious Second American Revolution!"

Accustomed to outbursts from her seventeen-year-old daughter, Mrs. Ben Boyd of Martinsburg (now in West Virginia) barely paused from her ironing to inquire, "And just what messages do you intend to deliver, and to whom, Isabelle?"

"Oh, Mother, you know that I have been associating freely with officers ever since Federal forces came here in July. You would be surprised to learn how much I have managed to pick up from their casual conversation. Now Fleeter is going to help me deliver my information to General Beauregard."

"You have no more sense than that horse of yours," her mother responded. "Beauregard will not listen to the chatter of a girl."

Having a vague idea that Company D of the Second Virginia Infantry, C.S.A., was somewhere in the Shenandoah Valley, the fair-haired, blue-eyed girl who had abbreviated her name to Belle jumped upon her horse and sped away.

She failed to make contact with her father's unit or with Beauregard, a Creole graduate of West Point whom she had come to idolize during her debut in Washington, D.C. Eventually, though, she did encounter a Confederate regiment. One of its officers took her to Turner Ashby, chief of cavalry and scouts in the force commanded by Gen. Thomas Jonathan ("Stonewall") Jackson.

Ashby listened to Belle Boyd's breathless account of her eavesdropping, jotted down a few notes, and promised that he would immediately take her name to his commander. "Keep up the good work," he urged. "One of these days, you will come up with something valuable."

Most messages sent from Martinsburg proved to be of no importance, but Confederate commanders were pleased to find that enemy lines could easily be penetrated. As a result, Jackson made Belle a semiofficial courier.

As military lines shifted, she traveled forty miles south to Front Royal to live with an aunt and increase the pace of her pro-Confederate activity. She was surprised and a bit dismayed when Gen. James Shields, leading Federal troops, occupied the town and chose to live in her aunt's hotel.

Dismay turned to glee, however, when she discovered that Shields and his aides frequently held conferences in his room. Creeping into the attic, Belle Boyd found a knothole in the floor above the room in which Union officers discussed their plans. Soon she enlarged the hole sufficiently to hear clearly when her ear was pressed against the floor.

Eavesdropping on Sunday, May 18, 1862, she was delighted to learn that scouts reported Confederate troops to be marching into the Shenandoah Valley. As a result of this intelligence, Shields gave orders to seize usable supplies in warehouses of Front Royal. Anticipating the probable abandonment of the town, he outlined a route of retreat.

Once she had discovered the enemy's plans, Belle Boyd moved into action. Mounting Fleeter as darkness fell, she rode fifteen miles to the nearest Confederate camp. After blurting out her intelligence, she climbed back into the saddle and returned home. Though never commemorated in poetry, her all-night ride made Paul Revere's accomplishment in the American Revolution seem easy by comparison.

Five days later, with Jackson's men approaching, Belle learned that Federal units planned to burn the bridges of the town as they retreated. Hastily weighing her alternatives, she decided that her horse would be a liability this time. Wearing a blue dress with a white apron, she dashed through the fields toward Confederate lines.

According to her own account of that memorable day, she

crawled along the tops of hills, sometimes climbing hastily over fences. Spotted by pickets of both forces, under heavy cross fire, she pulled off her sunbonnet and waved it vigorously to urge Confederates to "Come on! Come on!" Somehow, men of Hay's Louisiana Brigade and the First Maryland Regiment understood and responded. A force of about eight hundred men in blue was mustered, and many Federals were captured because Belle's action caused Confederates to move so rapidly that their foes did not have time to burn bridges.

Measured by the awesome scale of major Civil War battles, the brief engagement at Front Royal was insignificant. Yet Front Royal was Stonewall Jackson's first battle, giving him a victory that created fear in Washington. Because Jackson seemed poised to move northward very rapidly, perhaps even striking at the capital, Abraham Lincoln and his advisers had their attention diverted from the movements of George B. McClellan on the peninsula near Richmond.

In the aftermath of the engagement, General Jackson sent his volunteer courier a message of gratitude: "I thank you, for myself and for the army, for the immense service that you have rendered your country today."

Within the week, Jackson feared that he might be caught between converging forces of Union Generals John C. Frémont and Irvin McDowell. He fell back to avoid the trap, and Federal troops again occupied Front Royal. Almost at once, Gen. James Shields ordered Belle's arrest, the first of at least half a dozen.

Soon she was back in Washington, the city in which she had made her debut while a house guest of Virginia-born John B. Floyd, the U.S. secretary of war. This time, however, she attended no balls or banquets. Placed in Old Capitol Prison, she whiled away her time by using skills gained as a student at Baltimore's Mount Washington Female Institute. Standing at her window, she sang ballads and songs described by Leslie's Weekly as coming from "the Secesh Cleopatra, who is caged at last." So many persons began to gather every afternoon to listen to her sing that she was released after thirty days.

Back in Martinsburg by June 1863 and hailed as a heroine, she was again arrested. Described by the *Washington Evening Star* as "insanely devoted to the rebel cause," she was this time thrown into Carroll Prison. Here she managed to decorate her cell with Confederate flags smuggled in to her and attracted hordes of people by repeatedly singing from her window a ballad that began, "Take me back to my own sunny South."

In a desperate move to be rid of the jailed songbird, authorities took action not sanctioned by the U.S. Constitution and banished her to the South.

In March 1864 Belle Boyd boarded the blockade runner *Greyhound* at Wilmington, N.C. Bound for Europe, she later claimed to be bearing urgent letters from the Confederate president, Jefferson Davis. These communications never reached their destination, for her vessel was overtaken by the U.S.S. *Connecticut*.

In charge of the captives, Ens. Samuel W. Hardinge was himself soon captivated by the girl whom French reporters had begun to call "la belle rebelle." Disobeying orders, he took her to Boston and informally banished her for the second time—to Canada—knowing that from there she could

Belle Boyd [MATHEW BRADY SCHOOL, LIBRARY OF CONGRESS].

easily continue her journey to England. Her one-time captor joined her as soon as possible, and they were married in St. James Church, Piccadilly, on August 25, 1864.

Once Belle became Mrs. Hardinge, she converted her husband to the Confederate cause and persuaded him to go to Richmond to offer his services to Jefferson Davis. Less beguiling than his bride, Hardinge was unable to talk—or to sing—his way to freedom after being captured as a deserter. Shifted from prison to prison, he contracted a fatal illness.

Hardinge's death made the former Belle Boyd of Virginia, age twenty-one, the widow of a former Union officer from New York State. Stranded in London, she wrote *Belle Boyd in Camp and Prison,* a two-volume account of her exploits as a courier and spy. Income from the book was not adequate to support her, so she persuaded a noted theater director to give her the part of Pauline in the play *Lady of Lyons.* It had a successful run at the Theatre Royal in Manchester, after which she returned to America as an actress.

On Broadway she performed in *The Honeymoon* in 1868, but critics in her husband's city were less than kind to her. Smarting from their reviews, she renounced the stage to go on the lecture circuit describing her exploits. A reporter for the *Atlanta Constitution* who heard her years later exulted, "She is the original!"

At the Opera House in Atlanta and many other southern cities, she billed herself as the "Confederate Heroine BELLE BOYD of Stonewall Jackson and Shenandoah Valley fame." Audiences alternately shuddered and cheered as she rendered "her thrilling dramatic narrative, 'North and South—Or the Perils of a Spy.'"

Lauded by Douglas Southall Freeman as "one of the most active and most reliable of Confederate secret agents," Belle Boyd spent her final years telling her story in one-night stands. During the impoverished Reconstruction period, audiences paid twenty-five cents per ticket for an evening of entertainment by comedians, instrumentalists, and vocalists formed into a company by the girl who rode all night to alert Stonewall Jackson.

PART THREE

As Game as Fighting Cocks

Whether fighting on the battlefield or in conference rooms, Virginians by birth and by choice are notable for being "as game as fighting cocks." Their contests have been as varied as their backgrounds. Some fought for independence, others for conscience' sake, and still others for love of the Old Dominion.

Richard Henry Lee, as painted by Charles W. Peale [INDEPEN-
DENCE NATIONAL PARK].

8

Richard Henry Lee Fired Verbal Salvos at the King

"Does Peyton Randolph know that we have come together to talk?"

"Certainly not!" responded Richard Henry Lee. "You, Tom, of all persons, should know that. Randolph is bitterly opposed to making more trouble."

Thomas Jefferson nodded agreement, almost casually, because the three Virginians whom some of their colleagues called "conspirators" had already tested the president of the First Continental Congress. Turning to Patrick Henry, he inquired, "When we next convene in Carpenter's Hall, do you think Randolph will recognize you when you rise to speak?"

"He has no choice. Despite his personal views, I am persuaded that many delegates—perhaps a small majority—lean toward our views."

"Because you are already under suspicion by some, it may be imprudent for you to be first to speak of independence upon the floor of Congress," Lee suggested. "Randolph is bitterly opposed. Pennsylvania will hear nothing of it. Neither will anyone who is eager to placate the House of Commons. When the time comes, perhaps I should speak to the issue."

"You would be heard, I warrant," mused Henry. "But of us all, you probably have most to lose. Your Chantilly estate, obviously. Also the family business conducted by your brother, William, in London. Even Stratford could be endangered—"

"Surely not Stratford!" interjected Jefferson. "I have visited that hundred-room mansion built with imported bricks. It was put up by Thomas Lee, who was always totally loyal to England."

"But it is generally known that I am neither my father nor totally loyal," responded Richard Henry Lee. "There is much to lose, but more to gain. I say, sound the waters frequently and move forward as rapidly as the climate of the gathering permits. A few of us are regarded as radical. Some delegates are timid. A majority, I fear, are conservative."

On that note, the informal conference broke up. Since there were no rules governing the choice of delegates, each colony had proceeded independently. Both of New Hampshire's delegates voiced their indignation that Pennsylvania's outnumbered them three to one. North Carolina's three representatives, late in arriving, threatened to go home unless Virginia recalled four of her seven delegates. With Peyton Randolph in the chair, after days of wrangling, it was decided that each colony would have one vote regardless of the number of delegates sent to Philadelphia.

On October 8, 1774, a month into the Congress, a major rift developed. "Men talk gamely of supporting Massachusetts in her resistance," observed Lee, "but when it comes time to vote, they insist upon words that will cause no offense. Most of them are blindly loyal to the king—who is the real source of our troubles—and put all the blame upon Parliament."

In keeping with that observation, the Congress passed a resolution that said little:

> This Congress approves the opposition of the inhabitants of Massachusetts Bay to the execution of the late acts of Parliament; and if the same shall be attempted to be carried into execution by force, in such case all Americans ought to support them in their opposition.

Back in Philadelphia the following May for another session, the Continental Congress was faced with the fact that British soldiers had fired upon Americans at Lexington and at Bunker Hill. Lee's use of the word *independence* in conversation caused numerous colleagues to avoid him.

"They say they want conciliation, not confrontation," muttered the London-educated man from Westmoreland County. "But no one has yet shown how to conciliate a mus-

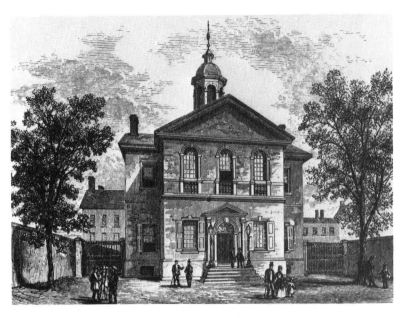

Carpenter's Hall, Philadelphia, where delegates drew up the Olive Branch Petition to King George III.

ket ball or a tax collector."

Over Lee's vocal objections, a dominant group of conservatives drew up a document that included a listing of some colonial grievances. But the subservient tone of the petition addressed to "Our Most Gracious and Christian Sovereign Lord" provoked the usually soft-spoken Virginian to anger.

"Too few Americans have spent years in England!" he exploded to men he felt he could trust. "They believe that by vowing their loyalty to George III, they can win his heart. Meanwhile, they blame lawmakers for our grievances. We can easily deal with the peers who make up the House of Lords and with the elected members of Commons. Our real enemy, whom we must sooner or later confront, is the king!"

Realizing himself to be hopelessly outnumbered, Richard Henry Lee voiced no objection to the idea of using Richard Penn as a messenger. A majority of those making up the Congress were confident that the king would welcome the grandson of William Penn. Surely he would then react positively to their message, they believed. Yet a handful of people made fun of the enterprise, calling the formal message of the Congress "an olive branch extended to a tyrant who is likely to gobble it up."

Penn reached London on August 14, 1775, anticipating an early and favorable audience with the king. But George III let it be known that he had no intention of receiving "a messenger of rebellion." Also, said the sovereign through his ministers, the humble petition drawn up in Philadelphia would not come to his attention through any channel.

Earlier, Richard Henry Lee had risked the confiscation of his estate by putting in writing his conviction that the closing of the port of Boston constituted a "most violent and dangerous attempt to destroy the constitutional liberty and rights of all British America."

Having become a close friend of John Adams, the Virginian went to the man from Massachusetts when word reached Philadelphia that the Olive Branch Petition had not even been read by the king. "I think it high time that each of the colonies begin to draw up plans to adopt independent governments," he proposed.

"Be wary of advocating independence," Adams warned. "Many ardent patriots avoid the word. Even my wife, Abigail, has written me that she fears the colonies would be incapable of self-government if suddenly granted independence.

"If you feel compelled to advocate independence, go about it indirectly. Plead, perhaps, the desirability—nay, necessity—that colonies enter into foreign alliances. Then point out that before such steps can be taken, they must form governments not wholly responsible to London. Be cautious. Remember that when you and George Wythe proposed a resolution saying that the king, not his ministers, was the author of our miseries, you achieved little except to create new opposition to our views."

Virginia patriots took a bolder stand. Urged by Lee, in a 1776 convention they adopted three radical resolutions. One suggested that each colony should form foreign alliances; a second called for independence; and a third proposed some sort of confederation among the colonies.

John Adams, who seconded Lee's call for independence.

Almost unanimously, colleagues agreed that Lee should bring these matters to the Continental Congress in its forthcoming session.

Speaking in a clear, musical voice, Lee instantly caught the attention of fellow delegates when he rose to speak on June 7. After preliminary remarks, he proposed that Congress go on record as supporting the view that "these united colonies are, and of right ought to be, free and independent states."

When Lee took his seat, Adams rose to second his proposals. In the hubbub that followed, it was instantly clear that many delegates were furious. But friends of Lee and Adams succeeded in having their names deleted from the journal of proceedings, a move designed to protect them from royal wrath.

After two days of heated debate, men opposed to independence succeeded in delaying a formal vote on the Lee resolution for three weeks. A special committee was formed: Thomas Jefferson, Benjamin Franklin, John Adams, Livingston of New York, and Sherman of Connecticut. Their task was to produce a formal statement giving reasons for supporting Lee's demand that "all political connection between these united Colonies and Great Britain is and ought to be totally resolved."

Urgently needed back home, the author of that statement left Philadelphia and returned to Virginia to help form a new government there. On July 1 the deadline for committee action expired. Against the fiery opposition of a group led by John Dickinson of Pennsylvania, Lee's resolution came to the floor.

To the consternation of conservatives, the call for independence won by a wide margin, setting the Congress on record as being in open defiance of the king and his ministers. John Adams rejoiced that in future generations, July 2 would be celebrated annually with fireworks.

On July 4, 1776, however, the special committee named to explain Lee's viewpoint brought to the Congress a formal document that was quickly adopted. A contemporary newspaper termed it "Mr. Jefferson's advertisement of Mr. Lee's resolution," but it soon became known as the Declaration of Independence. Largely shaped by Jefferson with some revision by the Congress, it was indebted to Lee for many of its emphases.

Paragraph after paragraph identified the king of England, not Parliament, as the implacable foe of Americans: "He has refused . . . . He has forbidden . . . . He has dissolved . . . . He has obstructed . . . . He has suspended . . . . He has plundered . . . . He has constrained. . . ."

Richard Henry Lee—no soldier—fired salvos of words rather than bullets. By doing so, he put himself in the dangerous position of being called by many of his contemporaries the "father of American independence."

9

Daniel Boone Never, Never Gave Up

"Shel-to-wee! Shel-to-wee!"

Inside the stockade at Boonesboro in Virginia's Kentucky country, Flanders Callaway warned his father-in-law, "Don't answer to your Shawnee name. We got plenty of trouble already."

"Gotta answer," responded Daniel Boone. "This time it is Black Fish, himself. I'm goin' out. If they grab me, I want you boys to slam the gate and start firin'. Just act like I'm not there."

Black Fish could not be ignored. Months earlier, the Shawnee and his warriors had gone on the war path. Furious at the treachery of British officials in Detroit, they seized white men at every opportunity. In February 1778 they captured Daniel Boone not far from the Blue Licks at which salt makers regularly camped.

"Your warriors are wearing British paint," Boone charged.

"No," Black Fish responded. "When the Redcoats came to us with guns and money, we would not take it as pay to fight you and the other Long Knives. Our great chief Cornstalk went to a fort of the Long Knives to talk peace. They took him inside. Then they killed him and his son. His spirit calls to us to take revenge. Tomorrow we will kill the men at the salt licks. Then we will take your fort and your women."

Boone managed to convince the war chief that Redcoats at Detroit would pay twenty pounds each for men taken alive, and nothing for those killed. He then led the way to the Licking River and ordered his riflemen to stack their weapons without resistance.

As the frontiersman later told the story, Black Fish immediately took a liking to him. Long before the party reached Detroit, the Shawnee had decided to make the leader of the Long Knives his adopted son. So when they reached the headquarters of Lt. Gov. Henry Hamilton, the Shawnee informed the British official that he had decided to keep Shelto-wee, or "Big Turtle," for himself.

At the Shawnee village of Chillicothe, Daniel Boone went through a ceremony by which he became a member of the tribe. Soon he was well liked, especially by the young squaws, he later reported. "But I was always careful not to beat the other Shawnees in shootin' matches," he said.

The vigilance of the Indians gradually relaxed, giving the tribesman by adoption an opportunity to escape on June 16. Somehow he covered the 160 miles to Boonesboro in just four days, never explaining how he got across the Ohio River, which was swollen by spring rains.

More than any other spot, Boonesboro was home to the man who took to the woods at age twelve. Situated on the south side of the Kentucky River and named for its builder, it was Virginia's first defensive post and settlement west of the Allegheny Mountains.

Some colonial leaders interpreted Virginia's charter to mean that her western boundary extended indefinitely. Others held that the colony's land claims—contested very early by Indians—ended at the Mississippi River, which few white men had then seen.

In London, more than three thousand miles away, the king and members of Parliament became concerned that "His Majesty's subjects in Virginia" might become rebellious if given too much freedom of movement. So an edict issued in 1763 forbade purchase of land from Indians and prohibited settlement west of the mountains.

Lord Dunmore, governor of Virginia, was too far from the seat of power to fear punishment for disobedience. Hence he organized expeditions against the Shawnees that brought military defeat to the tribesmen. Chief Cornstalk signed a treaty of peace in 1774 and under its terms ceded all claims to land south and east of the Ohio River. This region, which the Indians called *Ken-tuck-y,* or the "dark and bloody ground," became the focus of America's first speculative land development.

Richard Henderson and fellow investors formed the Transylvania Company and bought a vast tract north of the Cumberland River from the Cherokees. Henderson employed Daniel Boone to build the Wilderness Road through the Cumberland Gap to open the region to settlers. Pushing his road to the Kentucky River, Boone built Boonesboro. Soon he brought his wife and daughter there, the first white women to live in the extreme western region of Virginia.

Having invested so much of his life in Boonesboro, its builder was willing to die, if necessary, to thwart Black Fish on the day the Shawnee called for him to come out and parley.

At Boonesborough the fort was completed just in time to fend off the first of several Indian attacks.

Observers from one of Boonesboro's two blockhouses saw animated gestures that included much shaking of heads. Finally, to their surprise and relief, they saw Black Fish and Boone smoking the peace pipe. They did not know it, but their leader had persuaded his father by adoption that the settlement lay on land purchased from the Cherokees. Once Black Fish accepted that explanation, he offered to leave peacefully if the settlers would swear loyalty to the Great White Father across the sea and to his deputy, Henry Hamilton.

The whites accepted these terms, prepared a document to which they affixed their signatures, and nervously agreed to go outside the stockade for a ceremony of handshaking with the Shawnees.

Something—no one ever knew precisely what—went wrong during the ritualistic shaking of hands. Initially there was nothing more than a minor scuffle, but it soon mushroomed and shots were fired. Grappling with Boone, Black Fish was knocked to the ground and stunned. A Shawnee lifted his tomahawk to kill his white brother, but Big Turtle ducked and took a glancing blow to his shoulder. Then he and his men raced to the fort.

Once Black Fish recovered his senses, he examined the stockade from all sides and decided he would take heavy losses if he staged an all-out attack. Knowing that drinking water and food were likely to be scarce, he decided to starve out the settlers. That decision launched the longest American Indian siege on record.

After three days, most women and a few of the men under Boone's leadership were ready to surrender and take their chances. "No!" he shouted angrily. "Never! Never give up! We will show those redskins what we are made of before we are through!"

He put men to work splitting a tree trunk and then gouging much of the wood from the center of each half. With the sections bound together with iron stripped from wagon wheels, Boone made a crude cannon. It was fired only once, since it exploded at the instant it spewed rifle balls among the Indians massed together. What the attackers did not know was that the "big gun" was now useless, so they with-

Daniel Boone [James B. Longacre engraving]

drew to what seemed a safe distance.

Starting at the river bank, the Indians dug a tunnel hoping to enter Boonesboro without being exposed to rifle fire. They were within twenty yards of the stockade when heavy rains caused the roof of the tunnel to collapse. Two hundred Shawnees then abandoned their eleven-day siege and slipped into the forest, leaving Boonesboro badly scarred by fire arrows and barely standing.

Although the siege was a dramatic event of the time, it was barely noted in contemporary chronicles. Also, those who knew him best did not bother to preserve a record of Daniel Boone's life and accomplishments. Barely literate himself, he left nothing approaching an autobiography. Hence much that is known about him depends upon hearsay.

Born in Pennsylvania, Boone developed love for Virginia when with his parents he spent some time in the Shenandoah Valley at about age sixteen. Six years later, by then a married man, he fled from North Carolina to Virginia during the French and Indian War. Working as a wagoneer, he and George Washington were among 2,100 Americans who followed Gen. Edward Braddock to fight the French. In a disastrous encounter, Braddock was mortally wounded and

Boone was captured. Soon, though, he cut one of his horses loose from his wagon and made his escape.

Governor Dunmore later hired him to go into "the westernmost regions of the colony" to warn surveyors that Indians were on the war path. That expedition, and an earlier trip into what is now Kentucky, persuaded him that it was the land of opportunity. Once the American Revolution was fully under way, Virginia made Kentucky into a county and organized a formal military force with Boone as its captain.

When Boone's daughter was captured by the Shawnees, he staged a dramatic rescue, which James Fenimore Cooper recounted in his novel *The Last of the Mohicans*. Perhaps because he had accepted adoption by Black Fish, Boone was put on trial by his fellow whites. He refused to admit guilt and won acquittal and promotion to the rank of major.

Land claims of the Transylvania Company having been thrown out, Major Boone collected $20,000 and set out for Williamsburg to seek new titles. On the way he was drugged and robbed, forcing him to work years to repay others for their losses. Captured by the British at Charlottesville in 1781, he managed once more to escape.

When his claims for more than 100,000 acres of land were disallowed, he found himself as poor as he had been in boyhood. But he moved to Point Pleasant in Kanawha County (now West Virginia) to make another fresh start. Hunting in that region proved so poor that he followed the advice of his son and went to the Ozarks, where he once more lost his land as a result of defective titles.

Considering another westward move to make one more fresh start, he returned to his adolescent pursuits. Soon he was making what he called a "better than passable living" by shooting deer, beaver, and other animals to cure and sell their pelts. At age eighty-two, the man who opened Virginia's far west was not about to quit fighting.

It is understandable that when Lord Byron learned about some of Daniel Boone's exploits, he devoted seven stanzas of his poem *Don Juan* to him. Today the man who never gave up is popularly seen as the romantic epitome of America's early frontiersman.

10

George Washington's Longest Battle Was with His Own Countrymen

"My military career started when I fought the French and Indians," George Washington is said to have reminisced to intimates late in life. "At that time I was under the command of a distinguished British officer who did not dream that I would later fight his countrymen on many a field.

"My fortunate success in battle led Americans to insist that I place myself at the head of the new nation. Neither they nor I then conceived that my longest battle would be fought with my own countrymen, over the location of our Territory of Columbia."

Washington's "longest battle" began four years before the adoption of the U.S. Constitution. Mutinous members of militia companies staged a near-riot in Philadelphia, pointing muskets at members of the Continental Congress to emphasize their demand that they be paid long overdue wages. The frightened lawmakers hastily adjourned and moved their session to Princeton, New Jersey, where they considered themselves safe.

A special district with armed protection was essential to the future of the legislative body, its members decided. Hence on October 7, 1783, the Continental Congress adopted a resolution calling for erection of federal buildings "on the banks of the Delaware, near Trenton, or of the Potomac, near Georgetown."

Until then, George Washington had remained silent on the question of establishing a permanent seat for the central government the Founding Fathers hoped soon to create. Once Congress acted, the man who had led the Continentals to victory over the British spoke decisively.

"Our effort to establish a centralized government for the colonies has led Congress to six—no, seven—cities," he pointed out. "First it was Philadelphia, then Baltimore. Another session in Philadelphia was followed by a period at Lancaster and one at York in the same colony. Congress then returned to Philadelphia and has now retreated to Princeton."

Washington had no way of knowing that the site of the conclave would later be moved to Annapolis, Maryland, Trenton, New Jersey, and then to New York City; but he is said quietly to have helped circulate a satire by Francis Hopkinson who suggested building a capital on wheels "so that it may easily be transported from place to place."

Presiding over a 1787 convention called to revise the Articles of Confederation, George Washington helped guide delegates toward a radical decision. Instead of patching up the loosely drawn agreement under which the American Revolution was fought, they adopted an entirely new document, the Constitution of the United States. A clause in its first article stipulates that Congress shall have exclusive jurisdic-

George Washington compared the struggle over the site of a national capital with a long-drawn military campaign.

tion over "such district (not exceeding ten miles square) as
may, by cession of particular states and the acceptance of
Congress, become the seat of government of the United
States. . . ."

Having formulated a clear-cut plan to create a federal district as the site of government, matters might have proceeded swiftly and smoothly had it not been for sectional
rivalry and jealousy.

Philadelphia, considered by many Americans to be the
only possible city in which to put the new government to
work, abounded with Quakers. Since many of them were
"notorious abolitionists," southern delegates balked at the
prospect of seeing Congress meet always in the City of
Brotherly Love. New York City entered a strong argument for
being the home of the national lawmakers, but rural con-
gressmen let it be known that they feared Manhattan's
"money power."

Soon after the Constitution went into effect through
ratification by nine colonies, Maryland offered to cede ten
square miles to Congress; Virginia lawmakers followed with
a similar offer. At the national level, many top leaders made
no secret of their hope that the permanent seat of government would be somewhere within the Susquehanna River
Valley.

Seldom making a public statement that might add to sectional antagonism, George Washington never stopped fighting for a location somewhere close to the region he most
loved. Annapolis added to the uncertainty and confusion by
making a strong but somewhat ambiguous offer. New Jersey
heard of the Annapolis bid and promised to provide a free
site "anywhere in the colony."

Probably at Washington's instigation, the tobacco planters
of Virginia formed a coalition to top all earlier offers.
Provided it would become the permanent seat of the new
federal government, they said, Virginia would cede to Congress the town of Williamsburg, 300 additional acres, and
100,000 pounds in cash.

Their offer is a revealing clue to how battlefield victories
were less difficult than the laborious process of welding

thirteen independent colonies into one nation. So far, the English pound and its colonial counterparts dominated U.S. finance.

Two more years passed before the Continental Congress established the dollar as the U.S. monetary unit, stipulating that "the small coin be of copper, of which two hundred shall pass for one dollar." Most fledgling states, burdened by big war debts, were eager to see "assumption." That is, they wanted the emerging federal government to take responsibility for the debts of the former colonies. Anti-Federalists, outnumbered but vocal and powerful, were violently opposed to such action.

George Washington, who had had experience using spies to learn battle plans of the British, discovered that it might be possible to win over some anti-Federalists. As a result, his secretary of state called opposing factions together for a conference.

"Some leading Federalists may be willing to put their influence behind the move to fix the new capital on the banks of the Potomac," Thomas Jefferson suggested. "But they will do so only if some anti-Federalists will support Mr. Alexander Hamilton's proposal for assumption."

After considerable haggling, the first, and perhaps the biggest, political horse trade in American history was consummated in a nameless tavern that was a prototype of later "smoke-filled rooms." George Washington, who masterminded the deal, was quietly happy that the long fight about the location of the nation's capital was finally over, with the South being the clear winner.

On July 16, 1790, President Washington signed an act that called for Congress to remain in Philadelphia for another decade, then move to the Potomac River "at some place between the mouths of the Eastern Branch and the Connogocheague."

Having previously sold all of his holdings in the immediate vicinity, the president negotiated terms under which nineteen landed proprietors ceded their rights on March 30, 1791. Lots for public buildings were to be paid for at $125 per acre, with streets conveyed to the government without charge.

With the building of Washington well under way, a State De-partment spokesman called it an "ill-arranged, rambling, scrambling village."

By presidential proclamation, Washington established the terms of the sale. One-fourth of the purchase money was to be paid immediately by the treasurer of the United States, with "the residue to be paid in three equal annual payments, with yearly interest of 6 percent on the whole principal unpaid."

Virginia had previously donated a tract of six hundred acres, virtually worthless because it included only a few settlers. Alexandria, included in the original district and retained until 1846, was the largest town involved. On September 9, 1791, the first boundary stone was set in Jones's Point, Hunting Creek, Virginia.

Before construction began, Washington stipulated that "the outer and party-walls of all houses within the said City shall be built of brick or stone." In an additional bid to guarantee a city of pleasing proportions, he informed builders that "the wall of no house is to be higher than forty feet to the roof in any part of the city; nor shall any be lower than thirty-five feet on any of the avenues."

Thomas Jefferson, who later let it be known that he was displeased at not having been consulted, agreed with Washington's dictum that "no vaults shall be permitted under the streets, nor any encroachments on the foot-way above by

A home that stood near the middle of the site that became Washington.

steps, stoops, porches, cellar doors, windows, ditches, or leaning walls; nor shall there be any projection over the street, other than the eaves of the house."

A few southern leaders thanked George Washington for having taken time to select the site, by then usually called the District of Columbia. Many of his contemporaries never learned of the president's behind-the-scenes struggle that ended with satisfaction of his personal wishes.

Northern newspapers immediately dubbed the federal site the "Serbonian Bog." When power was officially transferred from Philadelphia to the city named for the man who picked its location, a Connecticut congressman described Pennsylvania Avenue as "a deep morass covered with elder bushes."

To jubilant political leaders of Virginia, Georgia, and the Carolinas, scathing criticism by the northern press did not matter. Philadelphia, New York, and other rich cities in the North had lost in the battle for the site of the national government. For good or ill, the capital of the United States was where it rightly belonged, within easy traveling distance of George Washington's beloved Mount Vernon.

11

Robert E. Lee Conquered the North Long after Appomattox

"Sit down, Colonel Lee, and make yourself comfortable. We have many things to discuss."

"I am due to see General Scott this afternoon, but until then, I have no engagement."

"Splendid! Let's begin by running briefly over your record. Correct me if I make an error."

Robert E. Lee nodded assent, having no idea why a founder of the Republican party and a trusted adviser to the White House should be so interested in him. Lee knew that Francis P. Blair, Sr., had played a major role—along with his sons—in preventing secession of Missouri. Was it possible that he had in mind a special mission in that state?

"Let's see . . . ," Blair began.

"Your father was 'Lighthorse Harry' Lee of Revolutionary fame. He fell into financial troubles soon after you were born, fifty-three years ago. After his death, much of the care of your sickly mother fell on your shoulders at Stratford, which I seem to remember lies in Westmoreland County."

Lee nodded, but said nothing.

"When you were approaching manhood, you realized that it would be impossible for you to attend one of Virginia's splendid colleges. This factor, combined with your admiration for your father, led you to seek appointment to the military academy at West Point.

"At the academy, you were not given a single demerit during four years. You graduated first in the class of 1828 and went with the Corps of Engineers."

"Second in the class of 1829," Lee responded.

Colonel Robert E. Lee, 1865

"Very well. That is immaterial. What matters is your subsequent record. By the time we felt it necessary to show the Mexicans what Americans are made of, you were a captain stationed in Texas."

"By that time, I had held the rank nearly a decade," his guest mused. "During peace time, promotions come slowly, if at all."

"All the more reason, Colonel Lee, for remembering that during the Mexican War you were associated with Winfield Scott. I believe that is when our general-in-chief said, 'When God Almighty got ready to make Bob Lee, he spit on his hands before he started work.'"

"I have heard some such statement, but I consider it to be barracks-room gossip."

"Nonsense! Now it appears we are about to enter into a conflict designed to deal with certain . . . certain rebellious . . . no, that is not correct. Certain *contentious* states. My son, the postmaster general, has heard other cabinet members speak of you. One of them said that when another conflict with England seemed likely, General Scott said, 'If the

British actually want war again, it would be cheap for our country to insure Lee's life for five million dollars.'

"That is not the reason for this conversation, however. Let me come directly to the point.

"A few days ago I spent an hour with the secretary of war. He is alarmed at the prospect of seeing a large army put into the field. As General Scott is now struggling with gout, Mr. Lincoln has authorized Mr. Cameron to determine whether you will accept command."

"You are sure that the president is behind this?"

"Positive. I see him frequently. He has mentioned you several times and says that no man in uniform is more deserving of the rank of general than you are.

"I see this has caught you by surprise. But you should have had an intimation that a proposal of some sort would be made. You were recalled from Texas rather suddenly and had hardly reached Arlington before you were promoted to your present rank."

"I did wonder," Robert E. Lee admitted. "But I decided that General Scott had some special assignment in mind. I am overwhelmed by the offer you have made. Give me time to find words."

After several moments of silence, Lee replied—according to Blair—in a single sentence: "If the Union is dissolved and the government disrupted, I shall return to my native state and share the miseries of my people and save in defense will draw my sword on none."

Remembering the conversation years afterward, Lee said he reminded Blair that he was personally opposed to secession but would find it impossible to play any role in an invasion of the southern states.

From Blair House on Pennsylvania Avenue, directly opposite buildings that housed the departments of state, war, and navy, the Virginian went to the office of Gen. Winfield Scott. Since Scott knew about Blair's mission, no time was wasted in reporting the offer and his reply. Reclining in a huge chair from which he could arise only with difficulty, the senior officer of the U.S. Army shook his head in dismay.

"Lee," he said bluntly, "you have made the greatest mis-

take of your life. But from the beginning of talk about you, I
feared it would be so.

"The contest may be long and severe, but eventually the
issue must be in favor of the Union. Officers who are resign-
ing with the intention of taking part with their states are
making fatal errors.

"But I suppose you will go with the rest. If you purpose to
resign, it is proper that you should do so at once. Your present attitude is an equivocal one."

"That is not my purpose, General Scott. The property belonging to my children lies in Virginia. They will be ruined,
if they do not go with their State. I cannot raise my hand
against my children."

Having rejected the offer of the enviable post,
Robert E. Lee returned to Arlington and resigned his commission with the hope that he would have no part in the
coming conflict. Within days, however, Gov. John Letcher requested him to take command of all Virginia forces. Appearing before the Virginia Convention to accept, he said in part:

> I would have much preferred that your choice had fallen
> on an abler man. Trusting in Almighty God, an approving
> conscience, and the aid of my fellow citizens, I devote myself
> to the service of my native State, in whose behalf alone will I
> ever again draw my sword.

After spending several months supervising Virginia's river
and harbor defenses, Robert E. Lee became special military
adviser to Jefferson Davis, president of the Confederate
States of America. He first took command of an army after
Joseph E. Johnston was incapacitated by a wound during the
1862 Peninsula campaign. Promptly named the Army of
Northern Virginia, most of its officers knew that their fifty-
five-year-old general, wearing a short beard for the first time,
had never commanded in battle.

During the next three years of conflict, in which his forces
were usually outnumbered two or three to one, Lee won a
permanent place in the ranks of America's top military
strategists. Revered by his men and civilians alike, when

surrender loomed he rejected a proposal by Col. E. P. Alexander.

"Instead of surrendering," Alexander urged, "disperse the regiments and let the men take to the woods with their weapons to work their way toward Johnston's army in Carolina."

"No," responded Lee, "such a course of action would turn honorable soldiers into guerrilla fighters. Though some could hold out for months or years, lonely and demoralized men would supply their wants by violence and plunder."

Having surrendered and accepted parole, the man who had turned down an opportunity to head the U.S. Army now rejected prestigious jobs in order to become president of Washington College at a salary of $1,500 a year. Before going to Lexington, he applied for amnesty and pardon, but he never received a reply. Although his beloved home, Arlington, had been turned into a military cemetery, he showed no signs of bitterness. Instead, he counseled students and faculty members, and Southerners in general, to leave defeat behind and devote their energy to being loyal Americans.

Only a few years passed before northern leaders, including former abolitionists, began expressing admiration for the

Robert E. Lee on the porch of his Richmond home shortly after Appomattox, flanked by Gen. Custis Lee (left) and Col. Walter Taylor (right).

The Virginia Memorial in downtown Richmond is surmounted by Robert E. Lee astride his famous horse, Traveller.

former head of the Army of Northern Virginia. His brilliant campaign tactics were studied in military academies in the United States and abroad as late as World War I. After his death in 1870, his memory was kept green by the Lee Monument Association, the Lee Memorial Association, and the Ladies' Lee Monument Association. His birthday, January 19, is a legal holiday in many states.

According to *The Encyclopedia of Southern Culture*, the postwar college president who refused to dwell upon old wounds and who was constantly working for reconciliation "became almost a Christ symbol, evidence that good men do not always prevail at first."

Having effectively conquered the North many years after Appomattox, only one victory remained for him. It came in 1975, when Congress restored the U.S. citizenship of the Virginian once charged with treason and never pardoned for his role in the Civil War.

PART FOUR

Mavericks, All

Some persons go through life accepting things as they are and seeking to blend into the crowd. Many of them rise to the top through accident, ability, conformity . . . or with a blend of these ingredients.

A rare few pay little or no attention to inherited ideas and practices and concentrate upon doing things the best way they can conceive. Of all persons, these mavericks are most likely to make enduring contributions to society and to be viewed by future generations in ways their contemporaries never glimpsed.

Vain and frivolous, King Charles II tried to award all Virginia to two of his courtiers.

12

Nathanael Bacon Refused to Submit

Nathanael Bacon, a well-educated member of Britain's landed aristocracy and cousin of Lord Chancellor Francis Bacon, died in Virginia as an outlaw. At his death followers of the twenty-nine-year-old rebel dumped his body in a river, then braced themselves to be punished for having followed him.

Bacon kept no diary; no painter captured his likeness on canvas; nothing resembling a "collection of Bacon papers" was ever assembled. Therefore information about him is fragmentary.

He is widely considered to have been the first American to have led armed resistance to the British monarch and his agents, and he enacted a short-lived set of his own laws that, on the surface, seemed to relieve some of the distress of middle-class and poor settlers who had been dominated by the rich. For a short time he was the most powerful man in Virginia.

However, neither his contemporaries nor later writers have made a full analysis of Nathanael Bacon's character and actions. He was successful in numerous raids upon Indians who were hostile to the colony, yet he burned Virginia's capital to the ground. He called himself "General by Consent of the People" and promised to throw off the yoke of tyranny from London, but he caused authorities to send the first British troops to be quartered in America at the expense of the people.

Whatever else the man educated at Oxford University may have been, he was a full-fledged maverick. He was so consistent in his refusal to conform that even when authorities changed their positions, he promptly altered his own views so that he might continue to protest and rebel.

Had Bacon not defied the colony's authorities and its laws, someone else would have done so. In 1676, the thirty thousand or so residents of Virginia lived in turmoil and uncertainty.

Bountiful crops had made tobacco plentiful, but since statutes required that it be sold only in England, prices had dropped in the saturated market. Also, at that time a colonist's chief means to personal advancement was through public office; but no new counties had been created in nearly a decade, and wealthy office holders in old counties usually managed to pass their positions along to their sons.

Internal problems were bad enough, but they did not concern the colonists as much as did the Indians of Maryland who were making raids into Virginia without being punished.

"How are we to gain satisfaction against these cruel enemies?" a frustrated member of the colonial assembly demanded. "We find ourselves handcuffed, with our feet shackled, for king and Parliament have decreed that Virginia militia may not set foot upon the soil of Maryland."

"Not all of our ills center in London," responded Nathanael Bacon. Not yet two years in Virginia and already owner of two plantations near the region that now includes Richmond, he pointed an accusing finger at Sir William Berkeley, the royal governor of Virginia. Now age sixty-nine, he had kept a firm grip upon the colony for years. Everyone knew that Berkeley was closely allied with the wealthy owners of large plantations, and he made no secret of his complete loyalty to King Charles II. Now Bacon accused him of having secret alliances with Indians.

"Beaver skins help to make a rich old man even richer," Bacon alleged. "In this colony, their value is second only to that of our splendid tobacco, and Indians bring in nearly all of the skins. Berkeley refuses to send me or anyone else against the Indians because he is lining his pockets with gold from the skin trade."

Having demanded from the governor a military commission he did not get, Bacon gathered a force of settlers and

Sir William Berkeley governed Virginia during most of two generations.

launched an unauthorized war against the Indians. Berkeley responded by proclaiming him a rebel and ordering his followers to disperse.

Contemptuous of any directive that came out of Jamestown, the insurgents won a number of skirmishes and drove the Indians back to the Rappahannock River. A new election having been called, voters of Henrico County elected Nathanael Bacon to the House of Burgesses. There lawmakers enacted a set of changes they called "Bacon's laws," then voted to make the rebel a general of the militia. Berkeley refused to sign and deliver the commission.

His refusal led Bacon to retreat to the Middle Plantation (now Williamsburg), where a band of five hundred cheering followers proclaimed him commander-in-chief of Virginia military forces.

When Bacon and his undisciplined little army appeared at Jamestown, a thoroughly alarmed governor pardoned him and delivered the prized military commission. Then on July 4 he penned to King Charles II a letter in which he commended to His Majesty's special attention a "zealous, loyal, and patriotic citizen—one Nathanael Bacon, lately of Friston Hall, in Suffolk, England."

Brandishing his commission to his followers, Bacon again marched against the Indians. Berkeley took advantage of his departure to issue a new proclamation. This time he branded his foe as a traitor to king and country.

When news reached Bacon that he was again an outlaw, he reputedly held a conclave of his own somewhere on the Pamunky River. In one of his rare statements, he said:

> It vexes me to the heart that, while I am hunting the wolves and tigers that destroy our lands, I should myself be pursued as a savage.
>
> Shall persons wholly devoted to their King and country—men who hazard their lives against the public enemy—deserve the appellation of "rebels" and "traitors"?
>
> The whole country is witness to our peaceable behavior. But those in authority, how have they obtained their estates? Have they not devoured the common treasury?
>
> I appeal to the King and Parliament, where the cause of the people will be heard impartially!

Berkeley, who had enough gunboats to control the rivers and seacoast, set about raising an army on the eastern shore of Chesapeake Bay. With five ships and ten sloops, he reached Jamestown in September 1676. There—for the third time—he proclaimed Bacon a rebel and a mutineer.

Leading his men in a hasty march against the capital, Bacon instructed them on the way to take as hostages the

In 1675 Nathanael Bacon used this captured mansion as headquarters.

wives of planters who were loyal to Berkeley. Tradition says he put some of these women in front of his own force when he appeared to demand the surrender of Jamestown. Berkeley issued an indignant refusal, but during the night his soldiers deserted.

Bacon and his men occupied the capital, consisting of sixteen or eighteen houses and a church, but he decided his men could not hold it if they were attacked by warships. So on a mellow September night, they torched the town and marched away, leaving only a few chimneys and the ruins of the church.

Except for the major waterways, the rebel was now master of all Virginia. Recognizing his numerical superiority, several groups of armed royalists deserted and joined his band. That encouraged Nathanael Bacon to make plans to cross the Chesapeake "to drive Berkeley and his royalists from the soil of Virginia."

He might have succeeded had it not been for the high price of living and fighting in swamps for week after week. His body covered with lice, the rebel developed "a most malignant fever" that claimed his life on October 11, 1676.

Whatever motives may have propelled the leader of the nation's first armed rebellion against authority, his death ended the movement. Governor Berkeley acted swiftly and sternly; within a few months, twenty-three of Bacon's chief followers were hanged. Nevertheless, what history books call Bacon's Rebellion led to the removal of Berkeley and to colonial reforms.

Also, long before the last insurgent was condemned and executed, a contingent of one thousand British soldiers had reached Virginia. Responding to news of rebellion, King Charles sent troops to restore peace. Since their orders did not stipulate a return home once the rebellion was quashed, the Redcoats were billeted in the homes of planters and settlers, the first contingent assigned to duty in a New World that in just one century would explode into a revolution that would change world history.

13

"When the Almighty Got Through Making Long Tom, He Broke the Mold"

"I am delighted to see you, ladies. What brings you to the Executive Mansion, half-finished as it is?"

"We represent the ladies of the new capital, Your Excellency, and we—"

"Hold on," interrupted Thomas Jefferson. "Though the title is well established, I abhor 'Your Excellency.' 'Mr. Jefferson' will do splendidly."

Taken aback, the spokeswoman of a self-chosen delegation hesitated momentarily.

"Very well . . . Mr. Jefferson, if you prefer. We have come to ask you to resume holding levees in the manner of President Washington. They are the most delightful social affairs of our government, and many of us looked forward to them from week to week."

Thomas Jefferson brushed a freckled hand over his reddish hair that was beginning to turn a bit sandy. Bending his head so that his soft voice might be heard more clearly, he enunciated carefully:

"Madam, I thank you and your colleagues. As a widower, I fully appreciate the way in which your presence graces this house. But I am republican to the core. It would not befit me to be present at weekly entertainments, and levees of the Federalist variety ill become our republic."

Tradition holds that having said no in as gracious a manner as possible, the man whose boyhood revolved about Shadwell, Virginia, sat down to dinner while still wearing boots and spurs donned for his late afternoon horseback ride.

Thomas Jefferson, third president of the United States.

George Washington's levees had taken place in drawing rooms from which chairs were removed so that no guest might sit in the presence of the chief executive. Dressed formally, the Father of His Country bowed stiffly to visitors but never extended his hand.

Thomas Jefferson caused tongues to cluck on July 4, 1801, when he ignored precedent and shook hands with about one hundred guests who had assembled in the Blue Room. To complicate matters, he flaunted the protocol in which "important" guests were given precedence.

Anthony Merry, minister to the United States from Great Britain, was among those scandalized by actions designed to stress the principle of "equality for all." Not only was rank ignored at receptions, he fumed, he and his wife had to sit down to dinner at a round table. "Mr. Jefferson," he reported, "seemed not to see Mrs. Merry. Instead of offering his arm to her, he led Mrs. Madison to a table which had no head or foot and on which was spread what seemed more like a harvest home supper than a dinner for diplomats."

Had Merry been in Washington earlier that year, he might have foreseen that things would change under Jefferson's administration. Instead of riding in an elaborate carriage to his inauguration on March 4, the president-elect had walked to the Capitol from Mrs. Conrad's boarding house to take the oath of office.

His predecessors, George Washington and John Adams, annually appeared before joint sessions of Congress to deliver addresses. Jefferson sent a written message to lawmakers, along with a note informing them that "circumstances rendered inconvenient the mode heretofore practiced."

When it came time for him to leave office, Jefferson was as unpredictable as he had been upon entering it. He arranged the first inaugural ball, which was held at Long's Hotel in Georgetown at seven in the evening, to honor the James Madisons.

Those who knew him intimately used different descriptive phrases. Some called him "a universal genius," thereby antedating modern analysts who term him "the last Renaissance man." Federalists railed at him as being "forever tossed by the wind, like a weather cock." But perhaps the best description came from intimates of the teenager whose enormous feet had signaled that he would grow to at least six feet, two inches in height. "When the Almighty finished making Long Tom," one of his comrades had observed, "he broke the mold and never made another like him."

Instead of making sure that his attire conformed to the dress code, Long Tom put comfort first. After having paid a formal call, Ambassador Merry wrote that he found the president "actually standing in slippers down at the heels, with both pantaloons, coat and under-clothes indicative of utter slovenliness and in a state of negligence actually studied."

That verdict may have been more nearly correct than the diplomat realized. Always zealous to stress that equality is the hallmark of a republic, the president may have practiced "studied negligence" so that others might know he viewed himself as no better than any laborer.

At a time when office holders were expected to exhibit strong religious ties, Jefferson calmly disavowed any affiliation. An exponent of the Enlightenment, he framed Virginia's 1786 Statute of Religious Liberty, causing critics to denounce him as an atheist.

With British-American ties deteriorating before the outbreak of the American Revolution, a majority of patriots favored conciliation with the mother country. Therefore, it was natural to turn to the man known for his independent way of thinking and acting to ask him to frame the Declaration of Independence.

Americans who remember little else about this "universal genius" are likely to have visited one or more of the buildings he designed. Monticello, his famous home, is the product of his skill as an architect. He also designed the Virginia capitol in Richmond and radically redesigned the Executive Mansion in which he spent eight years. Yet his crowning work as an architect is found in Charlottesville, where he designed the University of Virginia. Not content with planning its buildings and directing their construction, he drew up the courses of study and then selected faculty members. Early students were puzzled to find themselves required to choose their classes because, alone among universities, Jefferson's had no required "branches of instruction."

Long Tom collected plants, minerals, and bones. He played the violin for his own amusement and to the delight of guests. He advocated scrapping existing currencies in favor of a decimal system and use of the metric system of weights and measures.

Flaunting requirements that documents be hand written, he employed a Philadelphia invention whereby multiple copies could be made simultaneously. A pen in the writer's hand activated two or more other pens. The president of the United States often sat at his polygraph turning out four or five letters at a time while his pet parrot perched on his shoulder.

As an inventor, Long Tom was as versatile as he was talented. He constructed a clock with an outdoor and an indoor face, so he could see the time from his garden as well as from his library. He invented and was first to use the swivel chair, and he fixed Monticello's weather vane so it could be read from inside the house. He designed and constructed dumbwaiters for use in dining, and turnstiles on which to hang clothes that revolved into view at a touch.

Despite his insistence upon republican simplicity, he liked and served almonds from France, macaroni from Italy, and waffles from Holland. He was among the earliest of Americans to serve the new European delicacy called ice cream, and he imported fine wines from Portugal, France, Spain, and Italy.

This lover of fine things who insisted upon simplicity was seldom able to manage money well. By the time he vacated the Executive Mansion, he was deeply in debt; so he seized the opportunity to sell his library of 6,500 volumes to the nation, thus forming the nucleus of the great Library of Congress. Seldom solvent, he proposed to dispose of Monticello

Purchased and restored as a national shrine, modern Monticello is a monument to Thomas Jefferson's genius as an architect-builder, but not as a financier [THOMAS JEFFERSON MEMORIAL FOUNDATION].

by lottery. When the scheme failed, he left the mansion to his daughter, who auctioned off furnishings and sold the house to satisfy some of the claims against his estate.

Perhaps the most controversial of his many interests was a light-skinned slave, Sally Hemings. On her death bed, young Martha Jefferson had made her husband promise never to take another wife. Unable to marry again, say Fawn Brodie and other writers, Long Tom took his wife's half-sister to bed with him and during an affair that lasted thirty-eight years sired a number of children by her. Charged by political foes with immorality, he neither denied nor affirmed the relationship.

Yet the man of many facets spoke up firmly when presented with a crisis that he viewed as a great opportunity. His agents in Paris, Robert R. Livingston and James Monroe, were authorized to try to buy from France New Orleans and part of West Florida. Instead, they agreed to purchase the entire Louisiana Territory at about three cents an acre, truly one of the world's greatest real estate bargains. Even at that price, to which a surprised President Jefferson agreed, the total bill represented more money than there then was in the entire United States.

Long Tom confessed that he doubted the constitutionality of the purchase. Still, he pushed the deal to consummation and effectively doubled the size of the nation.

Clearly a genius and a maverick, the tall Virginian who followed no compass but his own is consistently ranked as one of the greatest presidents of the United States.

Jefferson's Monticello is located two miles from Charlottesville and is open every day except Christmas. For more information call (804) 295-8181. The University of Virginia at Charlottesville offers campus tours; call (804) 924-0311 for details.

14

John Charles and Jessie Frémont Never Conformed

Jessie Frémont, Virginia-born daughter of Missouri's Senator Thomas Hart Benton, barely glanced at the envelope addressed to her husband before opening it.

She scanned it hastily, then selected a courier to travel to the camp of explorer John Charles Frémont. Fearful that he might be stopped, questioned, and searched, she made him memorize the terse message:

> Do not wait for men or supplies. Move into the wilderness instantly. Never acknowledge that you have received this message.

At Westport, now Kansas City, her puzzled husband responded by giving orders to break camp and start west.

Long afterward, Frémont learned why his wife acted so impetuously. The official letter she had opened in St. Louis ordered Frémont to return to the river city. Not knowing of that order, Frémont penned from the right bank of the Kansas River a detailed report to Col. J. J. Albert, chief of the Corps of Topographical Engineers, U.S. Army. He was camped, he said, six miles beyond the western boundary of Missouri, "agreeably to your order to explore and report upon the country" between Missouri and the Rocky Mountains.

Back home two years later, still not knowing that he had proceeded against orders, he found himself lauded as the greatest explorer of the era.

"Frémont Reached the Great Salt Lake," a newspaper report exulted as a result of fragmentary information about the first part of his journey. That headline was correct, but it

John Frémont, the Path-finder, was the first Republican candidate for the U.S. presidency.

failed to give any hint about even more significant findings. Following the Snake River to the Columbia, he pushed all the way to Fort Vancouver. That exploit, alone, should have been enough to satisfy a man who, by virtue of his birth, was branded a maverick.

Mrs. Anne Whiting Pryor of Richmond became enamored of French-speaking John Charles Frémon some time in 1810. Not eligible for marriage, she went South with him. Labor pains forced the pair to pause in Savannah, Georgia, where a son was born.

Given the anglicized version of his father's name, John Charles spent much of his boyhood in Charleston, South Carolina, where his father taught French and his mother ran a boarding house. He won admission to the College of Charleston but did not last long there. In 1831 he was dismissed for "irregular attendance."

Self-study and classroom work had given him a good

grounding in mathematics, so he found a job teaching math to sailors aboard the sloop of war *Natchez*. Perpetually restless, he left the navy and joined the army's topographical corps to help survey Cherokee lands in North Carolina and Georgia.

Ever since he was old enough to hear stories about the past, Frémont had been eager to explore his Virginia roots. As a second lieutenant, he was assigned to Washington, sixty miles from his mother's early home. Soon, though, he forgot all about searching for his roots. Socialite Jessie Benton, a student at the boarding school of Miss English in Georgetown, caught his eye even though she was just sixteen and a self-described "tomboy."

Senator Benton and his wife, the former Elizabeth McDowell, exploded when Jessie told them that she wanted to marry the handsome young lieutenant. In addition to their own negative reactions, they urged, "You have to think of what your relatives in and around Lexington would say."

Convinced that they would never give their consent, at seventeen Jessie eloped with John Charles, more than nine years her senior. Once they were married, however, Senator

Mrs. Jessie Benton Frémont did not behave like the daughter of a U.S. senator.

Benton began using his influence to help his son-in-law. Thus Frémont came to head the 1842 party that explored much of the Rocky Mountains for the first time.

His second expedition, saved by his wife's quick action, brought him promotion to the rank of captain. Congress printed and distributed 10,000 copies of his report that included the earliest detailed information about many regions of the Great West.

Frémont's third expedition, also ostensibly designed solely for exploration, put him at the head of sixty expert marksmen. Since war with Mexico was increasingly probable, secret orders authorized him to convert his band into a military unit in the event of hostilities. Following instructions for once in his life, he led his men into California by way of the Donner Pass and reached Sutter's Fort.

In 1845, all California included only about eight hundred Americans who were barely tolerated by the three thousand Mexicans who owned and governed the region. News of the discovery of gold at Sutter's Mill had already created great excitement in the East. Concurrent with the arrival of Frémont's transcontinental band, a handful of early prospectors reached the region after having sailed around the tip of South America.

Mexican-American tension mounted rapidly, and the newcomers put their weight behind what they called their independent Bear Flag Republic. Frémont and his men approved of this move and perhaps aided it in spite of having been ordered out of the province by Prefect Manuel Castro. Returning after a brief exodus into Oregon, the explorers joined other Americans in celebrating July 4, 1846. Frémont organized and headed the California Battalion, and soon he pulled down the bear flag and hoisted the Stars and Stripes.

Soon he was made civil governor of California. In that post he represented the United States in negotiations that persuaded Mexico to cede the region. Many Americans who had not been interested in the acquisition of California now rejoiced that Frémont had named the Golden Gate and conquered Los Angeles while partly mapping the Pacific coast of the continent.

Ordinary folk were bewildered when they learned in 1847

that the great explorer was to be court-martialed for having squabbled with Gen. Stephen W. Kearney over lines of authority. The officers who sat in judgment weighed charges of disobedience, mutiny, and conduct prejudicial to military order.

He was acquitted of mutiny but found guilty of the other charges and was sentenced to dismissal from the army. President James K. Polk used his role as commander-in-chief to suspend the sentence in January 1848. Still, Frémont angrily resigned his commission and returned to California. There gold made him rich, and fellow citizens elected him to the U.S. Senate.

Men who had formed a new political party knew that no old-line leader would become their standard bearer in a national campaign. So they turned to Frémont, who in 1856 became the first Republican candidate for the presidency. Although soundly defeated by James Buchanan, he won enough electoral votes—114—to mark him as a man to be watched.

Abraham Lincoln, who kept a close eye on the unpredictable hero, believed he had found a way to put him where he could do no political damage. He made him a major general upon the outbreak of the Civil War.

Few of Lincoln's political judgments were so flawed. Sent to St. Louis, General Frémont itched for action. Without authorization, he made a daring effort to reach and defeat Confederates under Gen. Sterling Price, but he never contacted the enemy.

Perhaps he smarted at this loss of face, or maybe he followed his lifelong pattern of impulsively doing what he wished without waiting for orders. Whatever the motivation, he now took his boldest step ever.

Late in August 1861, the man popularly called "the Pathfinder" issued a proclamation. Under its terms, property of persons in rebellion against the United States of America was declared subject to confiscation. A second clause announced that slaves belonging to Missouri rebels were emancipated and made forever free.

At Chicago's Wigwam, many delegates to the Republican

Gen. John Charles Frémont was the first to proclaim that slaves were free [LESLIE'S ILLUSTRATED].

convention of 1860 had been chagrined to discover—too late—that their nominee for the presidency was no abolitionist. What's more, Abraham Lincoln refused to take a stand on the slavery issue and went to the White House pledged only to preserve the Union, regardless of what it might take to do it.

Desperately concerned about the border states in 1861, Lincoln was unwilling to take any step that might cause undecided voters to move toward the Confederacy. Consequently, he ordered Frémont to withdraw his emancipation proclamation. When the Pathfinder refused, his commander-in-chief rescinded the edict that freed most of the slaves in Missouri.

Leading Republicans called Frémont's policy the "only means of saving the government." To this verdict Lincoln responded bitterly: "On the contrary. It is itself the sur-

render of government." Lest anyone in or out of the military doubt his meaning, the president transferred Frémont to command of the mountainous anti-slavery region of Virginia (now West Virginia). There he was given inadequate forces, and his command was divided. Defeated by Confederates, he was made a subordinate to Gen. John Pope, a transfer that Lincoln correctly calculated would cause him to resign from the U.S. Army for the second time.

In 1864 he was nominated for the presidency for the second time when Radical Republicans said that Lincoln's re-election was neither possible nor desirable. Frémont's backers deserted him in exchange for the resignation of Montgomery Blair from the cabinet, and Lincoln was returned to the White House.

When postwar plans to build a railroad linking Virginia with California failed, the man who never conformed would have become impoverished had it not been for Mrs. Frémont. In a step that genteel ladies deplored, his Virginia-born wife offered her services to Robert Bonner of the *New York Ledger.* Surprisingly, at a time when few women of breeding earned money, Bonner paid her one hundred dollars each for a series of articles. Jessie Benton Frémont then began writing historical sketches, stories for boys and girls, and travel sketches. These led to her books *Souvenirs of My Time, Far West Sketches,* and *The Will and the Way Stories.* Then she helped her husband write his autobiography, in which he did not reveal that he had spent his entire life thumbing his nose at authority and convention.

15

Bypassing Established Ideas, Walter Reed Found the Cause of Yellow Fever

Camp Lazear, 9 12 '00.

Rejoice with me, sweetheart. Aside from the antitoxin of Diphtheria and Koch's discovery of the tubercle bacillus, it will be regarded as the most important piece of work, scientifically, of the era.

I do not Exaggerate, and I could shout for very joy that Heaven has permitted me to establish this wonderful way of propagating Yellow Fever.

Its importance to Cuba and the United States cannot be estimated. Major Kean says that the discovery is worth more than the cost of the Spanish War including lives lost and money expended.

Major Walter Reed's letter to his wife stemmed from a series of experiments that had demonstrated how yellow fever is transmitted. Until then, most scientists were convinced that contact with contaminated clothing, bedding, or body wastes triggered new cases of the often fatal malady. When early tests by a group Reed headed indicated that mosquitoes transmit yellow fever, he was widely ridiculed.

"They all call me a zealot and think I must be crazy," he confided to his wife. "I know that I am 'way off base,' as far as most authorities are concerned, but I also know that I am right."

Walter Reed's deviation from accepted patterns of behavior began early in life. Born at Belroi in Gloucester County, the son of a Methodist pastor, he spent several years in Farmville before moving with his family to Charlottes-

Maj. Walter Reed in the late 1890s [NATIONAL LIBRARY OF MEDICINE].

ville. Although he had studied only under his father and at a series of private schools, he entered the University of Virginia at sixteen and acquired his medical degree before his eighteenth birthday.

Dr. Reed did not try to establish a private practice since he knew that prospective patients would be wary of treatment by a youngster. So he enrolled at Bellevue Hospital Medical College in New York City, where he received a second M.D. degree two years later. Work for a hospital and for a board of health proved tedious and lacked opportunity for advancement, so at twenty-four he entered the U.S. Army Medical Corps.

"My career would have consisted of a monotonous round of routine assignments to frontier garrisons," he later said, "had I not decided to break out of the system by means of graduate study."

His request for a leave to seek further training was denied, but his superiors sent him to examine recruits in Baltimore and agreed to let him study bacteriology on the side. "It was a new and uncrowded field," he later commented. "When I completed my work with flying colors, they made me professor of bacteriology and clinical microscopy at the new Army Medical School . . . and at the same time made a major of me."

The outbreak of the Spanish-American War, with its hurried mobilization of troops, led to an epidemic of typhoid fever. Medical opinion then was that the disease was transmitted mostly by contaminated water. "I strongly doubt the truth of the established theory," Reed told his wife when he was made chairman of a committee to investigate typhoid. "Though I have no personal experience with the fever, I expect to show that water has little to do with its spread."

This time, he was wrong. With three colleagues, he made a study that was published in 1904. According to it, discharges from kidneys and bowels of sufferers, spread by water, flies, and even dust, can create an epidemic from a single case of typhoid. "Sanitation is the key to victory over the fever," Reed correctly proclaimed.

While Walter Reed was wrestling with typhoid in army camps on the mainland, more cases of yellow fever began to be seen in Cuba. Italian scientist Dr. Giuseppe Sanarelli published a paper saying that the dread disease is caused by *Bacillus icteroides.*

"Splendid!" exclaimed Surgeon General George M. Sternberg when Reed told him of the renowned specialist's findings. "Sanarelli's work will support my own ideas about *Bacillus X.* Find out all you can about *icteroides*, Major. I'll assign Carroll to work with you. Put everything else aside."

That directive led to an 1899 article in *Medical News.* Aided by James Carroll, Walter Reed put his career on the line. His report not only demolished the Italian's theory; simultaneously, it refuted ideas of the surgeon general.

"Sanitation has been shown to be the key to control of typhoid," high-level military leaders observed. "We're certain it is also basic to prevention of yellow fever. Since Dr. Reed made such a convincing case about typhoid, perhaps he is the man to reduce the toll of yellow fever in Cuba."

That reasoning caused Dr. Reed to be placed at the head of

a yellow fever commission that included Doctors Jesse W. Lazear and Aristed Agramonte, along with Carroll.

On the voyage from New York to Havana, Walter Reed was seasick the entire time. Weak from the loss of five pounds, he went immediately to Pinar del Rio and led a meticulous sweep of the community. Then he announced a radical break with established theories.

"We have heard a great deal about fomites," he said. "These agents are generally recognized as the vectors in yellow fever. Yet we do not know for certain that contaminated matter from fever victims is transformed into these things. Folk have tried turpentine, colonic enemas, and even cocaine in an effort to get rid of fomites. But no one has ever seen fomites under the microscope. I am not sure they exist. We must search elsewhere."

Earlier, a Cuban physician had suggested that yellow fever is transmitted by mosquitoes. He had no supporting laboratory evidence, and most physicians scoffed; but Reed did not. Considering alternatives, he decided to make field tests by which to determine whether fever is spread by fomites or by insects.

Gen. Leonard Wood, in command of U.S. troops in Cuba, authorized the building of Camp Lazear as a yellow fever center. Seven army tents erected there were of routine nature. But an "infected clothing building" was strange and different.

Ready for use on November 30, 1900, it was stuffed with material from hospitals in which yellow fever patients had died: underwear, towels, sheets, pillows, and blankets. A stove, installed to maintain a temperature consistent with tropical living, was the only equipment other than three beds.

Dr. Robert P. Cook and two other U.S. Army volunteers were told to fold, shake, and agitate clothing and bed linens to try to get many fomites into the air. Soon the stench grew so strong they rushed to the door to vomit. Then they returned, lay down on the beds, and used them for twenty consecutive nights.

"These brave men have demolished the fomite theory," Major Reed concluded when not even one man contracted

Maj. Walter Reed as seen through the eyes of a sculptor.

fever. "If there are such things as fomites, they do not serve to transmit yellow fever. We must now look closely at our little birds [mosquitoes]."

Some inconclusive tests had already been made, for it was easy to get volunteers. William H. Dean of Troop B, Seventh Cavalry, was the first to offer his arm to an insect believed to be infected. He stopped one morning to watch doctors at work and voiced surprise that they were "fooling around with mosquitoes."

"Will you give one of them a bite?" he was challenged. "Sure. There's nothing to be scared of," he responded.

Five days after having been bitten, Dean came down with

fever. Because he could have been exposed to fomites or other carriers, the case was considered inconclusive.

A series of controlled experiments showed that some mosquitoes that had bitten fever sufferers were able to cause new cases, while others were not. It took weeks to discover that about twelve days are required for the yellow fever virus to become potent within an infected mosquito, *stegomyia fasciata* (later renamed *aegypti*). An insect must take blood from a person whose fever is active and must "incubate" the virus it gets with the blood before it becomes loaded with the material that produces fever.

Before documenting the chain of events that cause an epidemic, Major Reed was invited to present his tentative findings to a meeting of the American Public Health Association. Most delegates regarded him as a troublesome nonconformist, so gave him just twenty minutes to speak.

Once Reed documented his conclusions, the medical community made an abrupt about-face. With a specific type of mosquito having been identified as the carrier, yellow fever was quickly reduced and all but eliminated among troops in Cuba. By 1905 it was eliminated from the Panama Canal Zone.

Shortly after Major Reed returned to his classroom at the Army Medical School, he took ill. Absorbed with teaching and research, he neglected warning signs; and by the time he let a fellow physician examine him, he was suffering from appendicitis too far advanced for surgery. He died at age fifty-one and was buried in Arlington National Cemetery. His widow, the former Emilie Lawrence, was awarded a pension of $125 a month.

Today, Reed's exuberant report to his wife is echoed throughout the world. The conquest of yellow fever is universally regarded as a milestone of modern medicine.

Unsolved Mysteries

It is one of those mysteries of life that some people and events that seem easy to understand in their own time become more difficult to comprehend as time passes. Rather than remaining in focus, the truth becomes blurred and it is difficult to determine what really happened, much less why.

On the other hand, still other people and events are puzzling even to those who are close to them. Time and distance do little to explain what they did or what happened.

Because part five contains both types of the mysterious, it is possible that at its conclusion you will find yourself with more questions than answers.

Situated in what is now West Virginia, remote Harpers Ferry
was a major military center.

16

John Brown Becomes More Enigmatic As the Years Pass

"Is that you, John Brown?"

"Nobody else!"

"I didn't recognize you," protested Frederick Douglass. "Under that old storm-beaten hat, you look like a fisherman."

"That was my purpose. I cannot take a chance on being recognized. Our plans are near fruition."

"Then you should have picked a better disguise," responded the black leader, a runaway from a Maryland plantation who had gained an international reputation as a leading abolitionist. "Here in Chambersburg, Pennsylvania, we don't see many fishermen. And this old quarry is no fit place to hold the conference you requested."

"Can't risk being seen together," white-bearded Brown responded. "Thank you for coming at my call. It is time for you to join my army. Sixty days from now—some time in October—we will strike the first blow."

"I thought you were planning to liberate slaves without bloodshed."

"That way would be better, but we don't know what the plantation owners and the militia will do. We have to be prepared, and they will be armed. So I have decided to move upon Harpers Ferry, in Virginia."

"Why that spot?" demanded Douglass. "There are many places easier to reach. And besides, there are few if any plantations in the mountains."

"No plantations, but plenty of splendid weapons. I already have more than enough for my own army. But when slaves rush to join us, they will need to be equipped, too.

Harpers Ferry holds an immense federal arsenal. With guns captured there, we can arm our men before we start toward Tennessee and Alabama."

"Hold on just a minute, John Brown! You keep saying 'we,' but I have not yet agreed to take part in your expedition. Until tonight, you said nothing about seizing weapons belonging to the United States."

"I want you by my side, Douglass," Brown is believed to have urged. "All is ready. A farm has been rented in Maryland. We will rendezvous there, just a short distance across the Potomac from the arsenal. Come with me!"

"An attack upon federal property," mused the man who previously had aided Brown in many ways, "will arouse the whole country, and your army won't last a week. Harpers Ferry may look good to you on paper. But when you go into the place, you'll be walking into a steel trap from which you'll never get out alive."

"Oh, no!" protested the self-proclaimed commander-in-chief of the army he proposed to raise in "a new sovereign state" in the slave-holding South. There will be opposition at first. So I will take plenty of hostages for self-protection. Once the slaves of Virginia hear of what is happening, they will flock to me like bees to a hive."

"No," Douglass said firmly, shaking his head. "This expedition is not for me."

Sunday, October 16, 1859, was cold and rainy at the Maryland farm rented by John Brown. After leading his men in Bible reading and prayer, he had them pile pikes and rifles into a wagon. An inventory taken the previous day showed there were weapons to spare: 198 rifles, 950 iron-tipped pikes, and 200 revolvers. Once the big wagon was loaded, two men drove it to a nearby schoolhouse. There, slaves who flocked from the hills would be armed upon arrival.

"All of the rest of you, follow me," Brown ordered, turning on his heels and climbing into a light wagon. Fifteen white recruits and four blacks clumsily formed a double file and started toward Harpers Ferry.

Situated at the confluence of the Potomac and Shenan-

John Brown before he grew his now-famous beard.

doah rivers about sixty miles from Washington and eighty from Baltimore, the town (now in West Virginia) was dominated by military facilities. In addition to the arsenal and armory, there was a private rifle factory. About half the 2,500 residents were black, but less than 100 of these were slaves. A majority of whites were federal employees or metal workers.

It proved easy to overpower guards and take possession of major buildings. Since the little brick fire-engine house was extremely sturdy and had few doors, Brown selected it for his headquarters. Several residents whom he had taken as hostages were herded into it, along with half of his men.

Some of Brown's soldiers were detailed to hold buildings, while others were dispatched into the countryside to bring in more hostages. Among the new captives was Lewis Washington, a collateral descendant of President George Washington.

Trouble started about midnight. Hayward Shepherd, a free black who worked as baggage master, started to walk along the railroad track. Almost in the instant that he was ordered to stop, he was shot and killed, the first fatality in the "war launched for the sake of black Americans."

Many residents fled from Harpers Ferry as soon as the shooting started. Those who remained pulled out their own weapons and at first light began firing at the raiders. Soon they were joined by bands of militia.

Still, John Brown was so confident that he sent to the hotel and got breakfast for his men and his hostages. By noon he was barricaded in the engine house along with eleven hostages and less than half his men. One of his sons lay dead, and another was wounded; both held commissions as captains in his army.

Word of the arsenal's seizure created fear in Washington. Col. Robert E. Lee, who was at Arlington on leave, was put in command of a body of marines whose mission was to repossess the town.

Except at the engine house, Brown's men were quickly overpowered. From his command post, he roared his refusal to surrender. Marines found a ladder and used it as a battering ram to burst into the tiny room in which four raiders still held eleven captives.

"Brown was the coolest and firmest man I ever saw," Lewis Washington said afterward. "With one son dead by his side and another shot through, he felt the pulse of his dying son with one hand and held his rifle with the other, and commanded his men with the utmost composure, encouraging them to sell their lives as dearly as they could."

Two of Brown's raiders died under bayonets of marines, who had been instructed not to fire their guns for fear of killing or wounding hostages. Himself slightly wounded, John Brown surrendered without a struggle.

It was the last thing he ever did quietly.

Gov. Henry A. Wise of Virginia, along with Sen. James M. Mason, soon arrived to interview him.

"I am an instrument in the hands of Providence!" Brown stormed. "God told me what to do!"

Questioned, he insisted that he financed the raid personally. "I cannot implicate others," he said. "It is by my own folly that I have been taken."

When John Brown was transported to Charleston for trial, a court-appointed defender was named. To the surprise of northern reporters who cried "Foul!" as soon as they learned that a Virginia attorney would represent the raider, Lawson Botts immediately tried to enter a plea of insanity.

His ploy might have worked had Brown not shouted his refusal to go along with it. Sentenced to death early in November, he asked to speak.

"I deny everything but what I have all along admitted: the design to free slaves.

"That was all I intended. I never intended murder or treason, or the destruction of property, or to incite slaves to rebellion, or to make insurrection."

Listeners who did not know that Brown and his sons previously had murdered five proslavery Kansas citizens who owned no slaves may have believed his passionate protestation. Throughout much of the North, a man who had shown himself to be a cold-blooded killer became an instant hero. Ralph Waldo Emerson lauded him as a "new saint [who] will make the gallows glorious like the cross."

Harper's Weekly said that "the insurrection was the work of a half-crazed white." Abraham Lincoln pointed out, "John Brown was no Republican, and not a single Republican has been implicated." But abolitionists raised their voices in a chorus of praise. Put to the tune of an old Charleston, South Carolina, hymn, "John Brown's Body" became their marching song.

Almost as soon as the hangman's rope was cut from Brown's neck, leading thinkers began debating his motives. Two schools of thought soon appeared. According to one, he was a stalwart Bible-reader and slavery-hater who gleefully went to his death knowing that he would be revered for what he had done.

Other analysts depicted him as irrational or even insane. According to this viewpoint, he had failed at everything he tried to do—as a candidate for the ministry, a land surveyor, land speculator, wool grower, and wool dealer. Emotionally unstable, he found his own brand of success by being hanged for an attempt to establish a new state populated by slaves given their freedom by soldiers of his army.

A third alternative cannot be ignored.

Despite his claim, most of his money and weapons came from prominent, wealthy abolitionists, at least sixty of whom gave him some support. Gerrit Smith, reputed to be the nation's largest landowner, was an enthusiastic backer. So was noted physician Samuel Gridley Howe. Almost with one voice, these men and their comrades, including the famous clergyman Henry Ward Beecher, insisted during the trial: "Do not use insanity as a defense. Let Brown die!" In their judgment, the raider's death on a Virginia gallows would do much to move North and South toward armed confrontation. Said the *Richmond Examiner*, "The Harpers Ferry invasion has advanced the cause of Disunion more than any other event since the formation of the Government."

Today, the mystery of John Brown is at least as enigmatic as it was in 1859. Was he a religious prophet ahead of his day? Was he a mentally unstable failure who found success on the gallows? Or was he the tool of wealthy and prominent men who were eager to have someone—anyone—show that war, and only war, would bring an end to slavery?

These questions could be more easily answered were it not for the raider's final act before mounting his wagon for the ride to Harpers Ferry. Having shaved his famous beard, he placed in plain view a trunk filled with letters and documents.

These records have been analyzed in detail only in recent times. Yet in the aftermath of Harpers Ferry, they implicated so many prominent abolitionists that some fled to Canada and England to avoid prosecution for having aided, abetted, and perhaps incited the raid that proved to be John Brown's path to martyrdom.

17

Battle Transformed Neurotic "Old Blue Light" into a Top Military Commander

"Open up! Open up this instant, or I'll kick the door down!"

Hammering with his fist as he shouted, James Walker was purple with rage. Prof. Thomas J. Jackson of the Virginia Military Institute opened his door slowly and deliberately, then stood in the threshold as his enemy brushed past him.

"You're responsible! Don't say you are not. I know the truth!"

"I believe you scored well in my natural philosophy class," Jackson responded in a fashion so calm that his words seemed almost mechanical. "In that class, I believe we posed the question What is truth? and found it hard to answer."

"You can't pull classroom stuff on me now. I'm out, for good. Both of us know that Old Blue Light is behind my dismissal, and that's the only truth I know."

Ignoring open use of a nickname widely circulated behind his back, the man whom many cadets also called Tom Fool Jackson was silent for a long, tense moment. "Let us both get down on our knees and pray for light," he suggested.

"Pray, my ass!" roared the student whose dismissal notice had come as a result of Jackson's initiative. "You can pray with the slaves. Nobody else would be caught dead at your Sabbath school class! What we need right now is action. Will you withdraw your charges and ask the superintendent to reinstate me at once?"

Wordless, Jackson solemnly shook his head and pointed to the door.

"You won't? Then take this, your high and mightiness!"

Withdrawing a glove as he spoke, Walker used it to slap his one-time mentor in the face. He did not have to issue a verbal challenge. The code of the time made it clear that the native of Gloucester City, Virginia, was challenging Jackson to a duel. Only eight years younger than the man he had come to hate, the disgraced ex-cadet was the larger and more powerful of the two.

Notoriously concerned about his physical condition and easily injured, Jackson rubbed his cheek for a moment. Then he turned on his heel, walked out of the room, and shut the door behind him without a word.

Nonplussed, James Walker strode to the inner door and lifted his fist to pound upon it. He paused, reflected for a moment, then lowered his arm.

"Old Blue Light won't stand up and fight! Old Blue Light is a coward! You can hide tonight, but some day we will meet again!" Walker then turned on his heel and left.

Told in connection with many a barracks-room brawl, doubtless embellished in oral transmission, that tale explains why a future general left V.M.I. during his senior year. His prediction about another meeting proved accurate, but it took place under circumstances neither man anticipated at the time Jackson refused to fight.

At the outbreak of the Civil War, Walker entered the Confederate service as captain of the Pulaski Guards. With his unit he performed admirably in the Shenandoah Valley, at Cedar Mountain, Second Bull Run, Antietam, and Fredericksburg. At Chancellorsville he so distinguished himself that he was made a brigadier general at the request of his ex-teacher who by then was famous as Stonewall Jackson. Upon Jackson's death, Walker was placed in command of the Stonewall Brigade.

While the reconciliation of one-time enemies, dramatic as it was, can be comprehended, the changes in Stonewall Jackson are as shrouded in mystery today as they were in the early months of the Civil War. What forces—internal and external—transformed an undistinguished and neurotic teacher into a totally self-confident military leader whose

Gen. Thomas Jonathan ("Stonewall") Jackson [W. G. JACKMAN ENGRAVING]

campaigns have been studied throughout the world?

Born and reared in what is now West Virginia, Tom became an orphan very early and was reared by an uncle. In spite of haphazard schooling, he managed to win an appointment to West Point, where he studied hard but had a mediocre record. After fighting in the Mexican War, he resigned from the U.S. Army to teach at V.M.I.

Before he reached the campus in 1851, rumors were circulating. At least one long-time staff member thought it strange that a man who planned a military career had become so ardent a religionist that he considered entering the ministry. As a deacon in the Presbyterian church, Professor Jackson read his Bible regularly and consulted it when facing a decision. His locally famous Bible class for slaves, which he launched soon after reaching Lexington, became so large that it was difficult to find a building in which to hold it.

"Religious ardor is questionable, but not necessarily bad," a member of the faculty reputedly said to the superintendent of V.M.I. some time in 1852. "What concerns some of us is this man's strange ways and his constant self-examination."

"Precisely what do you mean, sir?"

"I think you know. His list of ailments is a yard long: neuralgia, dyspepsia, curvature of the spine, rheumatism, chilblains, and God knows what else. His ears and his eyes give him a lot of trouble; anyone who spends any time with him soon discovers that. But why on earth does he try to improve his vision by dipping his head into a basin of cold water—eyes open—and staying under as long as he can hold his breath?"

"Honestly, I cannot say. I do know that he is a man of exemplary character, with a fine army record."

"Maybe something happened when he took off his army uniform. I find it hard to get along with him. Other faculty members will tell you the same thing."

"Perhaps," agreed the superintendent. "But we have entered into a contract. There is nothing I can do unless he commits a serious infraction of rules."

After a decade in the classroom in which he was distrusted by his colleagues and considered strange by his students, Jackson was abruptly thrust into a new role. As soon as Abraham Lincoln issued a call for volunteers to supplement the U.S. Army, Gov. John Letcher of Virginia made an urgent request of V.M.I.'s superintendent. "Pick your most advanced cadets. Put a man with military experience at their head," he urged. "Send them to Richmond at once. They are needed as drillmasters for our militia."

Chosen to head the body of students, Professor Jackson left home on April 21, 1861, and never returned. Commissioned as a colonel in Virginia forces, he fought for nearly two years without a furlough.

At First Bull Run, his unit's stout resistance to Federal advances is credited with having led Gen. Barnard E. Bee of South Carolina to exclaim, "Jackson stood like a stone wall!" Never mind that some later analysts have suggested that Bee was complaining about the Virginian's inertia, rather than exulting at his tenacity. Bee died on the field, so he had no opportunity to amplify a remark that on the spot created a legendary nickname. Soon Jackson's force was designated as the Stonewall Brigade, the only major Confederate unit whose nickname became official.

Many of Stonewall Jackson's subordinates disliked him

Early version of sculpture at Stone Mountain, Georgia, depicting Stonewall Jackson "riding forever with Lee and Davis."

intensely because he demanded the impossible from them while guarding his plans with great secrecy. Fellow commanders such as Brig. Gen. William W. Loring and Maj. Gen. Richard S. Ewell despised him or dismissed him as insane.

Yet the nondescript professor became a superb tactician. Over and over, he demonstrated that his men could and would perform feats that were considered impossible. In his famous Shenandoah Valley campaign, 20,000 men in gray baffled and frustrated the movements of 125,000 men in blue for six weeks. Stonewall Jackson rode along his lines, constantly urging, "Press on, men. Press on. Close up. Close up." So prodded, his men marched four hundred miles and fought five pitched battles without a rest.

At Chancellorsville, a brilliantly unconventional move saw his corps sweep around the Union flank and rout the Eleventh Corps. Late on the evening after his brilliant victory, he rode beyond his own lines to reconnoiter. Perhaps he failed to notice how rapidly the light was fading or did not remember that he had repeatedly ordered his men, "When you see strangers approaching, fire instantly and ask questions afterward."

In the dusky confusion, his own riflemen in Lane's Brigade picked him as a target. A ball shattered his left arm just below the shoulder while another passed through it near the elbow. A third shot hit the palm of his right hand. Seriously but not mortally wounded, he was momentarily near capture when Federals charged over the field where he lay. A countercharge enabled Confederates to recover their commander under heavy fire that killed a litter bearer, causing the wounded leader to suffer a bruising blow when he was dropped to the ground.

Surgeons pronounced their amputation of his arm successful and turned their attention to other casualties. That enabled a servant to follow Stonewall Jackson's orders concerning self-treatment for which he was noted. Draped perhaps for hours in cloths previously soaked in icy water, he contracted pneumonia and died on May 10, 1863, at age thirty-nine.

His lack of tidiness in appearance and his rigid moral views did not detract from his battlefield achievements. English admirers commissioned a bronze bust that was unveiled in Richmond in 1875, the first of many tributes that came to a climax with his election to the Hall of Fame of Great Americans.

His largest posthumous honor was yet to come. When members of a commemorative association succeeded in having one of the world's largest memorials blasted from the face of Stone Mountain near Atlanta, Stonewall Jackson was chosen to ride there with Robert E. Lee and Jefferson Davis.

If the Clarksburg native had any idea of what transformed him into a battlefield genius, he gave no hint to those who knew him best. Secretive to the point of withholding vital information from subordinates, upon reaching the field hospital after being shot, he issued the last of his characteristic orders: "Do not tell the troops that I am wounded."

18

The Civil War Began and Ended on Wilmer McLean's Property

"Though you are an unwilling host, you have provided a splendid meal. Thank you for it."

"My unwillingness stems from one fact, only, General Beauregard. In my absence, when you selected Liberia House for your headquarters, my slaves were hesitant to admit you. They yielded only because they saw your troops stretching as far as the creek."

Gesturing to punctuate rapid-fire speech, Wilmer McLean leaned forward and informed his guest, "I want nothing to do with war, sir, nothing!"

"Given a choice, I would want nothing to do with it either, Mr. McLean."

"But I have been told that you are a professional military man. Is it true that you are a graduate of the military academy at West Point?"

Pierre Gustave Toutant Beauregard nodded. "Class of '28. Second in the class, as a matter of fact. But that doesn't mean I enjoy fighting. When I went to the academy, our only enemies were Indians and Mexicans. Now we have the Yankees—all twenty million of them.

"But my feelings are beside the point, sir. I am under orders. A month ago, your own Robert E. Lee took command of Confederate forces. Knowing Manassas to be little more than thirty miles from Washington, he anticipated the invasion that is now under way.

"General Lee sent me to stop the enemy, but I am badly outnumbered. That is why, early tomorrow, I must begin selecting some strategic sites at which to station my men."

Beauregard yawned and stretched, rose to go to his upstairs

bedroom in the Virginia farmhouse, then paused and turned back to pose a question of his own. "My curiosity is aroused. Why do you call this place Liberia?"

"How did you discover its name?"

"When my aide stopped in the village to ask that the owner recommend a house suitable for my headquarters, he learned that there is only one in the vicinity: yours. He reported to me that I should look for Liberia, described as a large, two-story brick house having two chimneys and a cluster of out-buildings attached to it. We spotted it from a distance of half a mile. A lovely home, but an uncommonly strange name here in Prince William County."

"Loudoun County, if you please. And the name is not strange! It was selected by my father. As much as any man, he wanted to see the strife between North and South settled peacefully. My father has Quaker connections, you see."

"I have no quarrel with the Quakers, but you still have not satisfied my curiosity."

"Very soon after the American Colonization Society was formed, Father became an active supporter of it. About the time that I was born here in what was then Yorkshire House, he freed two of his slaves and sent them to Liberia with the very first contingent. He told me that his two blacks, along with eighty-six others, went there on the schooner *Elizabeth.* He considered renaming this residence for the ship, but instead decided to call it Liberia because he hoped that the establishment of the country of Liberia would resolve the slavery issue."

"He was not alone," mused Beauregard. "I have it from the highest authorities that Lincoln long favored gradual emancipation, along with transportation of free blacks to Liberia.

"But enough of Lincoln and Liberia. I am expecting the arrival of a Virginian within forty-eight hours. Perhaps you know of him: Thomas J. Jackson. Before he comes, I must select points at which to station our field guns, few enough, God knows."

Beauregard spent most of the next two days inspecting the region before deploying his entire force along an eight-mile stretch of Bull Run Creek, placing artillery at seven crossing points: six fords and a bridge. At McLean's ford, within the

Because artists issued sketches such as this, McLean's "portrait of the surrender scene" was a financial failure.

1,400-acre plantation of his host, he put two brass six-pounders and stationed three regiments and a company of cavalry.

Destined within hours to win the nickname "Stonewall," Jackson and his men reached Manassas after a forced march from Harpers Ferry. About noon on July 20, 1861, a wheezing little engine of the Manassas Gap Railroad arrived carrying the army of Joseph E. Johnston, the first fighting force ever to reach a battle site by train.

Union Gen. Irvin McDowell, camped nearby for two days with 12,000 raw recruits itching to fight, set things in motion about 2:00 A.M. on July 21. Hoping to envelop the Confederate left flank, he ordered his artillery to open fire at first light. Within minutes, a ball crashed through Wilmer McLean's kitchen.

Once infantry of opposing sides clashed, the battle became a furious melee. By the time Edmund Ruffin fired the last shot at men in blue who were retreating over a suspension bridge, it was clear that in the first real battle of the conflict Confederate forces had scored a glorious victory.

Mourning in Washington and rejoicing in Richmond brought no solace to Wilmer McLean. He surveyed the damage to Liberia House, rode over his battle-scarred fields still littered with the dead, and shook his head with sorrow and dismay. Situated near the opposing capitals, he reasoned correctly that the region in which he lived would see more war. To get away from it, he rode through much of Virginia seeking a refuge. When he found good land at the right price, he sold out—lock, stock, and barrel—and moved near a stage stop on the Lexington to Richmond route.

Nearly four years later, one of McLean's slaves brought him a strange message. A man in uniform—maybe a Confederate and maybe a Union soldier—had been seen riding toward Appomattox Court House waving a long pole. At the top of the pole was fastened what seemed to be a white towel. What on earth could it mean?

Wilmer McLean did not know that after having fought to a finish, the escape route of Gen. Robert E. Lee's army was blocked. In a desperate last-minute bid to avoid the trap set by Gen. U.S. Grant, Lee appealed to John B. Gordon of Georgia. Could he and his men cut their way through Federal lines, Lee wondered.

"I have fought my corps to a frazzle," Gordon answered.

Despondent, Lee told his aides that he had no alternative other than going to see Grant. He then dictated a request for an interview to discuss terms of surrender. Carried by a rider who waved a makeshift white flag, it reached Grant at Appomatox.

Grant turned to his secretary, Col. Ely Parker—a full-blooded Iroquois—and dictated a reply. He agreed to meet at once in a mutually convenient place.

Col. Charles Marshall, one of Lee's aides, galloped into Appomattox early on Sunday, April 9, 1865. Finding the courthouse locked, he asked resident Wilmer McLean to guide him to a suitable meeting place.

When McLean showed Marshall a dilapidated house bare of furniture, Marshall snapped that it positively would not do. McLean sighed heavily, then led the Confederate officer

Wilmer McLean House, Appomattox, as restored [VIRGINIA DIVISION OF TOURISM].

to a home not quite so splendid as Liberia House but resembling it in many respects.

Opposing commanders met in the parlor of the McLean home, talked for more than two hours, and agreed upon terms both felt to be honorable. Lee's men were allowed to keep their horses and side arms; then, as paroled prisoners, they were issued passes that permitted them to return to their homes.

As soon as the two commanders had signed the agreement, Federal officers began jostling for souvenirs.

"What do you want for the surrender table?" one of them demanded.

"It is not for sale," Wilmer McLean responded.

"Who said so?" responded Gen. Edward Ord. "Here! I have fifty dollars in greenbacks. You may as well take it. The table on which the surrender was signed is mine!"

The surrender scene as depicted by an artist, with Grant at the table seized by Ord as a souvenir.

Gen. George A. Custer hastily counted currency, then thrust twenty-five dollars into McLean's hand and made off with the table used by secretaries in preparing the documents. Within minutes, the surrender room was bare except for two chairs, which were soon seized by Federal cavalry officers.

Reduced to destitution, the once-thriving planter who hated war borrowed money to produce a lithograph depicting the surrender scene. Artists who had not been present that momentous day had already flooded the market with their imaginary sketches. Hence Wilmer McLean's did not sell, and his house fell into ruins.

Now elegantly re-created and refurnished, McLean House at Appomattox vividly symbolizes the long, dark night of the C.S.A. and the bitter winter of the man on whose property the war started and ended, both against his will.

Surrounded by Appomattox Court House National Park, the McLean House is closed only on federal holidays. For more information call (804) 352-8987.

19

Puzzled but Obedient, Hill Lamon Left Lincoln Unguarded

"Mr. Secretary, I am deeply worried."

"What troubles you this time, Hill?"

"The president has instructed me to spend several days in Richmond. If I go, I cannot protect him."

John P. Usher, U.S. secretary of the interior, leaned forward and inquired, "Precisely what am I supposed to do about it? Is it not common knowledge that I submitted my resignation more than a month ago?"

"Yes, it is known," admitted Ward Hill Lamon. "But I heard somewhere that it does not take effect until the middle of May."

"Heard somewhere? You got that straight from the president!"

Nodding assent, the marshal of the District of Columbia returned to the purpose of his visit. "You have considerable authority here in the capital. I beg you to use it to guard the president in my absence."

"I'm willing to do what I can, of course. But you and I both know that he is not particularly fond of me. Wouldn't it be better for you to stay by his side?"

"That's what I would like to do. But Mr. Lincoln has made up his mind. He remembers having sent me to Charleston before the firing started but has forgotten that I didn't do any good on that mission. Now he wants me to iron out some of the problems that block the calling of Virginia's reconstruction convention."

"Why doesn't he send someone from the department of state?"

"Since I was born in Frederick County, he believes that

Ward Hill Lamon was big, tough, and determined to protect the president.

leaders of the Old Dominion might listen to me. Besides, it is common knowledge that every black abolitionist in the country despises me."

"These are not persuasive reasons for sending you on such a vital mission," mused the secretary of the interior. "It seems to me that it would be better for you to stay in the capital and let someone else bargain with the rebels. Instead of accepting the burden of guarding Mr. Lincoln's life, I believe I prefer to try to have another agent sent to Richmond."

Far from satisfied, the man who for years had taken personal charge of Abraham Lincoln's safety tried to think of someone else on whom to call. Ward Hill Lamon correctly believed that Usher would do nothing.

Nearly a decade earlier Lamon had become a law partner of Lincoln when the future president was practicing in Danville, Illinois. He joined the new Republican party soon after it was organized and campaigned for Lincoln in 1860. When party leaders learned of assassination threats, Lamon was chosen to guard the president-elect during his journey to Washington.

Big and burly, the handsome Virginian became a familiar figure in the capital. As marshal, he liked to make spectacular arrests and execute orders of the circuit court. At many levees, he introduced visitors to the president.

Political foes derided Lincoln for putting a proslavery Virginian in a responsible position that kept him close to the chief executive, but the president did not waver. When plots were widely suspected in 1864, Lamon supervised the patrolling of White House grounds and himself slept next to the president's bedroom.

In Lamon's judgment, protection of the president became urgent near the end of 1864 when Horace Greeley's *New York Tribune* publicized a notice that had originally appeared in Alabama's *Selma Dispatch*. Apparently inserted by a Col. G. W. Gayle, an open letter offered a reward to killers:

> If the citizens of the Southern Confederacy will furnish me with the cash, or good securities, for the sum of one million dollars, I will cause the lives of Abraham Lincoln, William H. Seward and Andrew Johnson to be taken by the first of March next.

When the letter was brought to the attention of the president, he waved it aside. "Pluck a banjo for me, Hill," he requested, "and sing me a sad little song. What does anybody want to assassinate me for? If anyone wants to do so, he can do it any day or night, if he is ready to give his life for mine."

"Maybe so," admitted the burly Virginian, "but I would like for you to make me a promise."

"What is it?"

"I want you to promise me that you will not go out after nightfall unless I am at your side. And I particularly want you to promise that you will not go to the theater without me."

Abraham Lincoln hesitated, then shook his head. "I cannot promise," he said, "but I tell you what I will do. I'll do the best I can."

*   *   *

On April 5, 1865, the president was aboard the
U.S.S. *Malvern*. In the cabin of the warship he received
Gen. Edward H. Ripley, who wanted to arrest a former Con-
federate who had belonged to Rains's torpedo bureau.
According to Ripley, men of the secret Confederate organiza-
tion had been ordered to take action against "the head of the
Yankee government."

Informed of this and urged to speak with the one-time
rebel who had changed sides, Abraham Lincoln would have
nothing to do with the matter. "I must go on the course
marked out for me. I cannot believe that any human being
lives who would do me any harm," he said.

However, the next week the president told Hill Lamon
about a strange dream he had had a few nights earlier.
According to the chief executive, "I retired after having
waited for dispatches from the front. Once in bed, very late, I
began to dream.

"There seemed to be a deathlike stillness about me. Then I
heard subdued weeping that led me to climb from my bed
and walk downstairs.

"I went from room to room and saw no one but continued
to hear sounds of mourning. In the East Room, I met with a
sickening surprise.

"A corpse wrapped in funeral vestments lay on a cata-
falque that was guarded by soldiers. 'Who is dead in the
White House?' I demanded of one of them.

"'The president is dead,' he informed me. 'He was killed
by an assassin.'

"A loud burst of grief from mourners caused me to
awaken, but I slept no more that night. Though it was only a
dream, I find myself strangely vexed by it."

"Then, Mr. President, let me do all I can to ease your vexa-
tion," Lamon urged. "I will detail additional guards here at
the White House and put them on duty when you travel to
the Soldiers' Home. I will cast other duties aside and remain
with you day and night."

"No, Hill, that would never do. I would feel foolish surrounded by soldiers. And you have other things to do, some
of them for me, personally."

*   *   *

Laura Keene, star of Our American Cousin.

Keenly aware of Lincoln's dream and of his refusal to take extra precautions, the native of Frederick County repeated his concern when told to devote several days to the Virginia mission. Reminded that he was being given an order rather than a request, he stood hat in hand as he said goodbye to his friend.

"I don't understand why I must go," he told the president, "but I am accustomed to obedience. Please exercise extreme caution. Go out as little as possible, and never to the theater, while I am gone."

Silent for an instant, Lincoln responded, "I know you have my interests at heart. That is why you must go to Virginia."

Good Friday fell on April 14 in 1865, three days after Lamon was ordered to the former Confederate capital. Since the popular English actress Laura Keene was playing in *Our American Cousin*, the president and Mrs. Lincoln decided to go to Ford's theater that night. They invited Gen. Ulysses Grant and his wife to accompany them, but Julia Grant declined because she disliked Mary Todd Lincoln.

At the theater, no one noticed that a peep hole had been bored through the door of the box normally occupied by the president and his party. Action on the stage caught the attention of a substitute for the regular theater guard, and he deserted his post. After having peered through the hole bored with a gimlet that afternoon, John Wilkes Booth burst into the box wielding a one-shot brass derringer in his right hand and a steel dagger in his left.

Assassin John Wilkes Booth was depicted as inspired by the devil.

At a distance of less than five feet, he raised the derringer and sent a half-inch ball into Abraham Lincoln's head. It passed through his brain and lodged behind his right eye. Soldiers, policemen, the substitute guard, and a surgeon rushed to the side of the president; but from the first it was clear that he had no chance of recovery.

Word of the assassination reached Ward Hill Lamon in Richmond the following day. Cutting off his negotiations with Virginia leaders, he hurried back to the capital asking himself over and over, *Why on earth did he send me away, after so many warnings?*

Lamon's question is as profound today as it was in the aftermath of the assassination. Some historians theorize that the president was a fatalist who believed nothing could interfere with the course of foreordained events. A few have speculated that he harbored a death wish. Others think that with more than eighty threatening letters stored in a special pouch, all talk of danger came to be ignored. But why Abraham Lincoln ordered his long-time bodyguard to Richmond at the approach of Easter 1865 remains an unsolved mystery.

20

Is Christ Church an "Architectural Stonehenge"?

"Events of March 30, 1988, are etched into my memory; I will never forget them."

Interviewed two years later, Stephen Stewart's voice became tense with emotion as he recalled what he saw that day in Christ Church, Lancaster County:

"I went to the churchyard to see grave sites and wandered into the church almost as an afterthought. The church is the finest piece of religious architecture from colonial times. It was neglected for years, and restoration was not completed until 1971.

"Knowing that some of its features are unusual, I thought it would be interesting to look them over. But about 5:10 or 5:12 P.M. my eyes fell on the area that includes the altar. After that, I saw nothing else.

"There's an oval window in the west wall, and sunlight was streaming through it. About the time I realized that I was seeing a solar spotlight, I looked more closely at the wall upon which it played. A beam formed by interaction of window and sun fell squarely upon the Ten Commandments above the altar. Suddenly it hit me. *We're close to Easter. I wonder where that light from the window will be then?*

"Curiosity took me back the next afternoon, and it was easy to see that the oval beam had moved. It did not stop; every day I saw it inching its way forward."

A longtime and ardent member of the British Horological Society, years before Stewart developed keen interest in time, sundials, and antique clocks. He knew that the date of Easter is determined by a complex formula that causes it to vary by thirty-five days.

Wondering whether there could be a correlation between the moving sunbeam and the approaching holy day, he consulted a 1928 edition of a prayer book. In it, he not only found a table for calculating holy days; he also discovered that "mean Easter" is a precise rather than a movable date. Every year, it falls on the fourteenth day after the vernal equinox.

"You had better believe that when mean Easter arrived, I was standing in Christ Church watching like a hawk," he says. "Already, the beam of light from the sun was very close to the cross. I think I was not greatly surprised—more elated than astonished—to see that the light landed squarely on the altar at 5:13 P.M., capturing the cross in its glare."

Stewart does not wait to be questioned but hastens to express his conviction, "A single unusual phenomenon, though 'neat' and unlikely to be purely accidental, is meaningless. To mean something, it must be linked with other phenomena." So he made it his business to try to learn if Christ Church has more than one unusual trait.

His findings came to the attention of the staff of the National Geographic Society. They sent a writer-photographer team to investigate.

As reported by the news service of the Society, Joy Aschenbach found Christ Church to be an architectural gem. Now a registered historic landmark, it was described by her as "an imposing mausoleumlike brick structure built in the form of the Greek cross." Also, there is no record concerning the designer and no copy of original plans.

Residents of tiny Weems, where the church stands, think that it was built by opulent Robert Carter about 1732. Owning 300,000 acres of land and 1,000 slaves, "he wanted to imitate and to outdo Bruton Parish Church in Williamsburg."

There is no doubt that the builder "outdid" the church in the colonial capital in many respects, but imitate it he did not. None of the puzzling features of Christ Church were copied from Williamsburg.

Once Stephen Stewart discovered an apparent link between the structure of the church, the movements of the sun, and the mean date of Easter, he began looking for other phe-

Having neither steeple nor cupola, cruciform Christ Church is said by many to look more like a mausoleum than a church [Virginia Department of Conservation].

nomena and soon found them.

He discovered that the beam of light that first caught his eye again reaches the cross exactly fourteen days before the autumnal equinox. Then he found that the north wing, so located that it always casts a shadow, functions as a sundial on the north lawn.

Spring is separated from summer by precisely ninety-four days, and there are ninety-four days between summer and fall. Having noticed that a shadow cast from the cornice of Christ Church moves up or down the exterior west wall at approximately the rate of one brick per day, Stewart decided to count the horizontal rows.

"Tears came into my eyes when I reached the eighty-third row and realized that I was close to the top," he remembers. "For a moment, I was too overcome with emotion to continue counting, certain in my heart that I would find the total to be ninety-four. When I confirmed that number, I al-

A sunbeam illuminates the cross fourteen days after the
spring equinox and fourteen days before the fall equinox
[CINDY YAMANAKA PHOTO © 1988 NATIONAL GEOGRAPHIC SO-
CIETY].

most fell off the ladder. 'My God!' I said to myself, 'This
building is a calendar!'"

Once he was convinced that the design and alignment of
Christ Church made it "an architectural Stonehenge," Stewart began examining other features. He spent so much time
measuring and counting that those in charge of the structure
instructed him not to enter it again without written permission.

With national attention aroused, a formal statement was

prepared. According to it, the policies of the vestry of nearby Grace Episcopal Church—caretaker of the mystery-shrouded structure—"do not support certain allegations purporting that Christ Church was built or intended to function for any purposes other than the worship of God."

If that was indeed the only function the builders had in mind, some observers wonder how so many numerical features came to be included.

There are twelve months in a year and twelve positions on a timepiece. Christ Church has twelve walls and twelve windows.

Though not present in the noted Williamsburg church, Christ Church has a row of dentils, or small rectangular wooden blocks, at the point where the wall meets the roof. From front to rear, there are exactly as many dentils as there are days in the year; along the sides there are 104 dentils, twice the number of weeks in the year. Carved into the wooden sounding board over the pulpit there are 208 dentils or 52 x 4. The west door has 26 panels, one-half the number of weeks in a year. A count of all dentils at the cornice shows them to number 938, a sum exactly equal to twice the number of days in a year plus four times the number of weeks. A water table around the exterior of the building is fashioned from 417 bricks, equal to the number of days in a year plus the number of weeks.

Danville building constructor P. L. Anderson, a specialist in Georgian architecture, studied Christ Church after learning about some of its features. "It was carefully designed to coordinate three dimensions," he concluded. "Height of the oval window, angle of the sun, and distance of the oval window from the cross are coordinated so that sunlight bathes the cross during the Easter season. Change one of at least seven dimensions of the building, and the phenomena that anyone can see would not exist."

Rickey W. Parker, a Chatham-based computer expert who produces programs that map the universe, was initially skeptical. At Anderson's request, he used his software to position the church against the sky. That is how he found Christ Church to be aligned about three and one-third degrees west of true east-west. "No other alignment would produce the observed solar phenomena," he says. "Shift the alignment or move the church a few miles, and there would be no Easter effect."

Stewart, Anderson, and other analysts believe they know why architectural plans have never been found. They suggest that plans by Sir Christopher Wren could have been used without his permission.

According to this view, Christ Church may have been built by Robert ("King") Carter's father, John. A distressed Royalist who sought refuge in Virginia about 1649, John Carter was a native of Buckinghamshire, England.

Christopher Wren, who grew up near Stonehenge and had a lifelong fascination with astronomy, learned a great deal about designing buildings from an uncle, Matthew Wren, a distinguished architect and Anglican bishop. As late as 1636, the bishop employed a curate named John Carter, who disappeared about the time that Matthew was brought up on twenty-two charges during the regime of Oliver Cromwell.

There is no known evidence that the John Carter who was associated with the teacher of Christopher Wren was the same John Carter who settled near the confluence of the Rappahannock River and Chesapeake Bay, about eighty miles east-north-east of present-day Richmond. But can the names and circumstances be purely coincidental? Is there a possibility that a Royalist linked with Christopher Wren brought along a set of the great architect's special plans when he fled to Virginia?

Church authorities and others who challenge the idea that Christ Church is an architectural timepiece indebted to Christopher Wren insist that the burden of proof is upon Stewart and his fellow believers.

Right they are. But they have offered no tentative explanation for the solar and numerical aspects of the building that are far too numerous to be dismissed as products of chance. As a result, Christ Church sits in lonely splendor as an unsolved mystery of the Old Dominion.

Situated near U.S. Highway 3 and Virginia routes 200 and 222, Christ Church is well worth a visit. Parish officials do not, however, welcome questions concerning its possible role as a calendar and a timepiece.

PART SIX

Pace Setters and Record Makers

Just as the original colony surpassed all other English ventures on the North American continent in size, so have Virginians led the pack in many fields of endeavor. From education for blacks to oceanography, from exploration to building scenic highways, men of the Old Dominion have left their marks upon the modern world.

Not all pace setters and record makers are included here. Tales of women, fighting men, mysteries, and mavericks involve many other notable first events and achievements.

James Madison was forced to become the first and only chief executive to go into battle while in office.

21

President James Madison Took to the Field of Battle

Writing to her friend Hannah Gallatin late in July 1814, first lady Dolley Madison said:

> Washington City is in a state of perturbation. Such a place as this has become! I can't describe it. I wish we were at Philadelphia.
>
> Among other threats, [the Federalists] say that if Mr. Madison attempts to move from this House, in case of an attack, they will stop him and that he shall fall with it.

One of several letters penned from the Executive Mansion during a time of increasing tension, this one did not reach its recipient until early August. By that time matters were much worse.

"[The secretary of war] Armstrong does nothing to protect the capital," President James Madison told his wife. "I have moved heaven and earth trying to persuade him to act, but he continues to insist that the British view Baltimore as a prize of such value that they will not come here."

"Some say that your Secretary of War has cataracts," responded Dolley Madison. "I think it far more likely that he willingly put on blinders the moment they hitched him to De Witt Clinton's cart."

"Political considerations cannot be ignored, but the truth is that I have selected an incompetent," the president responded. "Armstrong does have strong Federalist leanings. They make him the target of abuse from our own Democratic-Republican leaders. Yet even they do not think that he would willingly turn this city over to the British.

"No, this time the general is not being swayed by hope that he can put Clinton into this mansion. He really believes that we are in no danger."

"Then what hope do you have, if Admiral Cochrane brings his men here? How long ago was it—six months—when we first heard of a plot to burn the city?" Mrs. Madison asked.

"Much more than six months," answered the president. "At least a year, about the time that we began to feel the effect of the British blockade.

"That blockade has been ruinous to Virginia. They are hurting badly, even in Port Conway where I was born. Three years ago Virginia exports amounted to nearly five millions of dollars. Products sent abroad this year will barely reach seventeen thousand dollars in value."

"Then maybe General Armstrong is right. Perhaps the blockade is so successful that the British won't bother with anything except our best seaports."

"Maybe," admitted the beleaguered president. "But the king and Parliament are still smarting from our Revolution. Nothing would please them so much as seizure of the capital so that they could torch it and put the 'makers of Revolution' in their proper place."

"Your argument sounds convincing," his wife admitted. "But there's little that the two of us can do tonight. Let's try to get a little sleep and hope that General Armstrong is right."

Some observers had already agreed that if James Armstrong should be proven wrong, it would be too late to act. Madison had authorized the use of fifteen thousand militia for defense of the capital and surrounding area. Gen. William H. Winder, commanding the military district of Maryland and Virginia, initially seemed ready to heed the president. However, after several talks with Armstrong, he decided it would be premature to call a force of that size to arms. So he placed only three thousand members of the Maryland militia on active duty.

A few days after the defense of the capital was arranged, lookouts on the Virginia coast spotted "a vast array of sails." Soon veterans of European campaigns began debarking from fifty-one British transports.

Suddenly alarmed, Winder sent urgent messages to the governors of Virginia, Maryland, and Pennsylvania. "All available militia must set out for Washington City without delay," he ordered. Nevertheless, he knew that British forces could cover the sixty or so miles to the capital while militia units were still being mobilized.

Many of the British advanced up the Patuxent River in small vessels. Others formed marching columns whose officers saw to it that they neither pressed ahead nor fell behind the flotilla of small craft. On August 22 the combined river and land forces reached Nottingham, halfway from their starting point to their target.

By then certain that his worst fears would be confirmed, Madison ignored his secretary of war who continued to insist, "Baltimore is the place they will strike, sir."

"I see that I must serve as commander-in-chief in the field, rather than in my office," Madison told a group of hand-picked aides. "Therefore, I want you to move heaven and earth to concentrate troops here. Try to get as many as possible who have had battlefield experience," he urged. His own military background consisted of drilling and target practice as a member of the Orange County militia during the American Revolution.

"Assemble as many wagons as you can get together quickly," he ordered. "Find tarpaulins to cover them. Then put our chief state papers into linen sacks and pile the wagons high with them. We must not—we dare not—permit our Declaration of Independence and our sacred Constitution to fall into British hands."

Returning to the Executive Mansion, the president embraced his wife before telling her that his duty lay with the troops. They made plans for evacuation of their residence, if necessary, and talked of places where they could meet in Virginia should they be separated for any length of time.

"Why you?" Dolley Madison is said to have demanded as the time of her husband's departure drew near. "Even Mr. Washington was not subjected to enemy gunfire while exercising the office of president. He was a veteran of many a hard campaign, and you have never heard the whistle of enemy bullets. Must you go?"

Nodding wordlessly, the president of the United States mounted his horse and kicked the animal's flanks. As he rode away, he turned and shouted, "Take good care of yourself . . . and of the Cabinet papers!"

Anticipating that defenders of the American capital would have burned bridges across the Potomac River, the British struck at Blandensburg, Maryland. Here the river was so shallow that it could be waded.

During two days of chaotic struggle, in which channels of communication were so poor that defending units often found themselves isolated, James Madison rode the battle lines. He wore out two horses, once found himself briefly trapped between opposing forces, and remained in a frenzy of concern about his wife.

The first British troops to swarm into Washington City broke into the House of Representatives. With a grizzled sergeant presiding, they enacted mock legislation that called for the burning of the city. By the time the Capitol was ablaze, other units had entered the Executive Mansion from which Dolley Madison had fled only a few hours before they arrived. Following instructions, she had taken important papers and a portrait of George Washington with her.

Smashed furniture in the Oval Room served as kindling. While the fire was getting under way, a Redcoat found and seized a bundle of letters written by James Madison. Another discovered one of the president's hats and took it as a souvenir. Soon flames roared through broken windows and the burning roof, permanently blackening the exterior walls of the mansion.

Virginians later insisted that the glare of fires set in the capital by the triumphant British could be seen forty miles away. But to the chagrin of the victors, the chief documents of the United States, major treaties, and congressional records were nowhere to be found. Although the British did not know it, these papers were aboard a train of twenty-two wagons headed, by order of James Madison, to Leesburg and safety.

Revelry of the soldiers of occupation was soon interrupted

by a violent storm. Roofs were ripped off houses, and trees were uprooted. Even a few three-pound cannons were overturned by force of "a most tremendous hurricane."

To many of the British, the storm appeared to be an act of God. Those not inclined to believe in providential intervention soon decided that the Americans were likely to regroup and strike before they could organize again. So Admiral Sir Alexander Cochrane decided to pull out of the still-smoldering city, leaving behind about two hundred dead and one hundred seriously wounded men.

Having been separated from his wife for about thirty-six hours during the four days he was constantly in the saddle, combat soldier James Madison found Dolley at a Virginia safe-house. Ignoring taunts of his political foes who blamed "little Jemmy" for the debacle, he refused to move the government to Philadelphia. However, the damage to the Executive Mansion was so great that he and his wife never returned to it. With the exterior walls given many coats of paint to cover the fire-blackened bricks, for the first time it became known as the White House.

Had Madison's subordinates listened when he first voiced warnings, it is unlikely that Washington would have been captured and burned. Because they did not heed him, the civilian from Virginia became the first and only chief executive to face enemy fire while in office.

James Madison's home, Montpelier, lies four miles southwest of Orange, on State Route 20. Tours are offered by the National Trust for Historic Preservation. For information, call (703) 672-2728.

At 129 Caroline Street in nearby Orange, the James Madison Museum offers four permanent exhibits. For information, call (703) 672-1776.

22

A Stagecoach Accident Helped Motivate "the Pathfinder of the Seas"

"I suppose all of you know why I am here instead of upon the deck of a man o' war. You have seen me walk with a decided limp. It was brought about by a permanent injury to my right knee. Otherwise, I would not now be taking over this depot."

Matthew Fontaine Maury, age thirty-four, surveyed crew members of the U.S. Navy's Depot of Charts and Instruments one by one. "If any of you imagine that my infirmity will make me severe, you are right. Aboard ship, I was known as a hard taskmaster. Here, I shall expect much more from you than I would expect from ordinary seamen."

"Will our work be changing?" a veteran of the depot inquired. "Under Mr. J. M. Gillis, it has been much the same from year to year."

"I am not Mr. Gillis. I am Matthew F. Maury. Your work will be changing a great deal. In addition to your accustomed tasks, you will be expected to help gather and analyze a great many new reports."

"We are a branch of the United States Navy, not bookkeepers," the questioner objected.

"Correct. But when it comes to winds and currents, warships and mercantile vessels are alike. All are often at the mercy of the elements."

Maury paused and tapped his leg. "As surely as this knee will handicap me for the rest of my life, the winds and the currents will handicap ships' captains, so long as they know nothing about them except what they have experienced or have heard from others. Together, we are going to change that."

Within weeks, the man born near Fredericksburg designed a special logbook. Printed copies were offered to ships' captains without charge, on condition that recipients promised faithfully to make notations. Once one of the strange little books was full of entries, it was to be returned to Washington.

At age five, Matthew was taken by his parents to a new homestead in Tennessee. There he studied in rural schools for half a dozen brief terms, then entered Harpeth Academy near Franklin. Inspired by an older brother who was a naval officer, the adolescent secured a midshipman's warrant in 1825 at age nineteen.

Without having had a chance to gain his sea legs, he was ordered aboard the U.S.S. *Brandywine.* Maury soon learned that the vessel would convey the Marquis de Lafayette to France, who was going home after his famous return visit to the nation he helped to liberate.

A second and much longer cruise on the *Vincennes* took the young seaman completely around the globe. Promoted to lieutenant in 1839, he was sent to the South Seas—or Pacific coast of South America—as astronomer for the navy's "exploring expedition." By then married to the former Ann Hull Herndon of Fredericksburg, he established their home in the town near which he was born.

Back from the South Seas, Maury visited his parents in Tennessee. While returning to Virginia, he rode in a coach pulled by nervous young horses. When they bolted at the scream of a wildcat, the stagecoach was tipped over. Two passengers suffered only minor injuries, but when a surgeon examined Maury's knee he said, "You'll be lucky if you manage to get by without a peg leg, young fellow."

When amputation was advised a few days later, Maury shook his head grimly. "Not unless gangrene sets in," he stipulated.

After weeks of convalescence, he limped aboard another vessel to assume his duties. Soon, though, he found that the lurching of the ship often caused him to sprawl upon the deck. His senior officers advised him to ask for shore duty, and when he failed to do so, they acted for him. Hence he was under no delusions when he took over the Depot of Charts and Instruments; the rest of his naval career would be spent on land. Because he had general knowledge of astronomy, it was logical to put him at the head of the new Naval Observatory as well as of the charts and instruments depot.

Long before his special logbooks began coming back to him, Maury had a message for every mariner who would listen. "Don't wear yourself and your sails out trying to fight the winds and the currents," he urged. "Learn how these forces behave, then cooperate with them and put them to work for you."

Data about the regions most frequently plied by U.S. seamen accumulated more rapidly than Maury had expected. Just four years after launching his "fishing expedition for new information," he published a compilation of findings called *Wind and Current Chart of the North Atlantic*. Follow-up studies made him supremely confident by 1851. "If mariners will follow my charts and the explanatory sailing directions that accompany them," he said, "they can greatly reduce the time required to pass from New York to Rio de Janeiro."

Some veteran salts—civilian captains as well as masters of naval vessels—scoffed at taking advice from "a land-locked sailor whose observations come from a point on the Potomac River." But mariners who tried his plan soon found that it enabled them to cut forty or more days from the long New York to San Francisco voyage.

Observations of cooperating captains, rather than first-hand experience, convinced the Virginian that there is a huge and relatively constant flow of water from the Gulf of Mexico to England and Europe. He called it "a great river in the sea," but lived to see it universally known as the Gulf Stream.

His 1855 book, *The Physical Geography of the Sea*, received world acclaim as the first textbook of oceanography. Now the world's great waterways constituted a distinct branch of scientific discipline.

Cyrus Field therefore considered it logical to consult the man who walked with a limp when he considered linking North America and Europe by an undersea telegraph cable.

Maury quickly labeled the idea as feasible, then cooperated with Field to select the season in which work would be least likely to be halted by great storms. While working on this project, he found and charted "the Telegraphic Plateau," now called the Mid-Atlantic Ridge.

High-ranking naval officers who were displeased that a man who had spent only a few years at sea was winning world recognition acted to put the upstart in his place. When Congress enacted legislation to create a board "to promote the efficiency of the navy," Matthew F. Maury's name was on the list of officers to be reviewed. His leg injury having rendered him unfit for sea duty, members of the board reported, Maury was to be given an involuntary leave of absence.

This decision may have stemmed in part from earlier activities of the now-famous student of the oceans. Writing under the pseudonyms of Harry Bluff and Will Hatch, he had published a dozen articles in the *Richmond Whig and Public Advertiser*, a newspaper readily available in Washington. Scathing criticism of a secretary of the navy and his chief aides was not forgotten when congressional action gave naval brass an opportunity to review Maury's record.

If the naval establishment cared little for "the father of oceanography," merchants and seamen and their political

"Pathfinder of the Seas" Maury is represented by a bust in the Virginia Hall of Fame.

allies cared a great deal. Legislatures of seven states passed resolutions demanding that he be restored to active duty. President James Buchanan took these signals so seriously that he restored Maury to active duty by executive order and at the same time promoted him to the rank of commander.

Abraham Lincoln, Buchanan's successor, had been elected on a campaign pledge to save the Union, no matter what he must do to accomplish that goal. On the day Lincoln took the oath of office as president, Commander Maury wrote, "The line of duty, therefore, is to me clear—each one to follow his own State if his own State goes to war; if not, he may remain to help on the work of reunion."

On April 20, 1861, three days after the secession of Virginia, the man from Fredericksburg resigned from the U.S. Navy to take command of the defense of Virginia's harbors. As a commander of the Confederate navy, he invented and tried to put to use an electric torpedo. Sent to England in 1862 as a special agent of the C.S.A., he managed to secure a number of warships for the Confederacy.

When the war was ended, Maury was at sea, stranded there because C.S.A. representatives abroad were excluded from the general amnesty proclamation. He worked briefly for the emperor of Mexico, attempting to expand a colony of ex-Confederates there. After another stay in England, Maury—by then more widely honored abroad than at home—returned to Virginia.

Beginning in 1868, he served for four years as professor of meteorology at the Virginia Military Institute in Lexington. When he died, he was buried between the tombs of Presidents Monroe and Tyler in Richmond's Hollywood Cemetery.

In 1930 the largely self-educated oceanographer who spent most of his life on land was elected to the Hall of Fame of Great Americans. In a volume devoted to the lives and achievements of great scientists, Isaac Asimov points out that Matthew Fontaine Maury's "forgiveness by the United States [for his activity as a Confederate] is total. At the Naval Academy at Annapolis there stands Maury Hall, named in his honor, even though for four years . . . he would have destroyed the American navy if he could."

23

Little Books of William McGuffey Shaped the Mind of Nineteenth-Century America

"I am a teacher of children with little or no competence in the field of philosophy," William H. McGuffey reputedly wrote in reply to an invitation to join the faculty of the University of Virginia.

"Whether you know it or not, you are teaching a philosophy of life to tens of thousands of children," he was informed in reply. "In Charlottesville you will have a free hand to teach moral philosophy in any fashion that you may choose."

Legend says that it was the shadow of Thomas Jefferson, rather than the prestige of membership in a distinguished faculty, that brought McGuffey to Virginia. On arrival he found that the influence of Jefferson, whom he revered, was to be found everywhere. Although he had been restless and constantly on the move early in his life, he spent his last twenty-eight years in Charlottesville, teaching until shortly before his death in 1873.

Born in a Pennsylvania log cabin, at age two William moved with his parents to another log cabin near Youngstown, Ohio. Opening of the "Connecticut Reserve," which offered free land to veterans of the Indian wars, was the magnet that drew the family to the Buckeye State.

McGuffey attended the intermittent sessions of rural schools and showed an astonishing capacity for learning and for memorization. Hence, his father worked extra hours on another man's farm to send the boy to a Latin school operated by the pastor of a Presbyterian church.

Before age eighteen, William was noted for his ability to quote entire books of the Bible and passages from great writers. He studied briefly at the Old Stone Academy in Darlington, Pennsylvania, before moving on to Washington College. Because he took time out to teach in rural Kentucky schools to earn the money for his own studies, graduation did not come until he was twenty-six.

Word of the bright young teacher-student came to the attention of the trustees of Miami University. Therefore, before he had received his diploma, he was invited to teach languages in the school at Oxford, Ohio. During the decade that he spent in the little college town, he was ordained as a Presbyterian minister, which enabled him to develop his own sets of moral principles and rules while preaching weekly in Darrtown, four miles away.

Leaders of Cincinnati College persuaded McGuffey to become its president, hoping that he would be able to solve its financial problems. He was unable to achieve that goal and saw the institution close its doors during the fourth year of his administration. However, while he was in Cincinnati, he organized an association to promote education and, with a few colleagues, established the public school system of Ohio.

With the West expanding rapidly, Cincinnati became a new center of the publishing trade. Winthrop B. Smith, of Truman and Smith, became convinced that the West would purchase and use grade-school textbooks in quantity, provided that they conveyed values associated with farm life, patriotism, and religion.

Catherine Beecher, sister of the future author of *Uncle Tom's Cabin,* seemed to Smith to be eminently qualified to turn out such textbooks. After she listened to his proposal, she turned him down. It seems that she may have suggested that he make contact with an exceptionally able teacher: William H. McGuffey.

"Of course I am interested!" McGuffey responded when approached by the publisher. "I have spent my adult life in the classroom and the pulpit. I have preached more than three thousand sermons without writing out one of them. I rely entirely upon my memory, you see."

Not convinced that a man so overtly religious would be able to write school books, Smith conferred with his partner.

Soon he offered McGuffey a contract for production of six volumes: a primer, a spelling book, and four reading books. If written to the satisfaction of the firm, he said, a royalty of one thousand dollars would be paid for the entire lot.

Drawing upon his prodigious memory and a sheaf of brief sayings he had used to teach the alphabet, McGuffey worked rapidly, always in the same fashion. Thus when he came to lesson #46 of the *Second Eclectic Reader*, he hesitated only a moment before writing:

> Seven-year old Ralph Wick went walking with his mother. She loved him very much, in spite of the fact that he cried easily and loudly.
>
> His mother gave him a nice red rose, and he was glad. Then he saw that she had a white rose. When his mother did not give it to him, Ralph screamed and kicked.
>
> That had no effect upon his mother, so Ralph snatched the white rose from her hand. Thorns on the rose tore his hand and made it sore.
>
> After that, when Ralph screamed for something he did not need to have, his mother pointed to his sore hand.

Almost all schools in the West were private, and few had money to spend on anything but essentials. But the reading books, initially not identified by the name of their author, were instantly successful. At the celebration of his fortieth birthday in 1840, McGuffey was proud to tell relatives and guests that his "little books" were selling nearly five hundred thousand copies annually.

Over a period of seventy-five years, the five "McGuffey Readers" made millionaires of Truman and Smith, and eight successor publishers. Yet when a *Rhetorical Guide* was needed in 1843 as an addition to the series, Winthrop Smith offered only five hundred dollars for the manuscript. Neither then nor at any other time was McGuffey greatly interested in money. When invited to join the faculty of the University of Virginia, he did not even inquire about the salary.

In contrast, he was barely settled in the position that would give him something he valued more than money—stability—before he launched a crusade to establish a pub-

William H. McGuffey, professor of moral philosophy, University of Virginia.

lic school system in Virginia. After years of hard work, he saw that dream realized.

During more than a quarter of a century in Charlottesville, McGuffey constantly revised and sometimes enlarged his now-famous readers. Almost without exception, teachers and parents were delighted with them. Short words and simple sentences made for easy reading, and best of all from the standpoint of adults, nearly every page carried a clear-cut lesson that was designed to help boys and girls be very, very good.

A typical selection dealt with two boys who quarreled over a nut. A larger and older boy volunteered to serve as referee. He cracked the nut and gave half of the shell to each small boy. Then he kept the kernel for himself as payment for having settled the quarrel.

In another reading lesson, small Bessie persuaded her Aunt Annie to allow her to hunt wild flowers to plant in a garden. Busy digging violets, dandelions, and other flowers, Bessie forgot about the time.

When she heard a bell calling her home, Bessie did not waste a second. She dropped her flowers and ran home so that dear auntie would not have to wait for her.

Adults who browsed through an *Eclectic Reader* usually gave enthusiastic recommendations to friends and relatives. As a result, by the turn of the century combined sales of volumes making up the set had topped 100,000,000 copies.

Advertised almost entirely by word of mouth, reading books that taught moral values as an extra were firmly entrenched in the nation's private schools when tax-supported institutions began to emerge. In his Charlottesville office, the author smiled triumphantly when he learned that the new public school systems were as enthusiastic about the *Eclectic Readers* as were the private systems. Eventually McGuffey's books were formally adopted in public schools of thirty-seven states.

Small enough to fit comfortably into a child's hand, the

"As soon as Bessie heard the bell, she dropped what she was doing and ran home so auntie wouldn't have to wait."

thin volumes taught a great deal more than reading. Their moral and cultural emphases helped to shape the lives of generations of boys and girls. No other textbooks ever issued have had quite the same influence as did McGuffey's.

About 1920, teachers and parents began to pride themselves upon being more sophisticated than those of the past. Inevitably, they turned away from the *Eclectic Readers* to textbooks considered more up to date and less moralistic in tone.

Later, however, the pendulum swung again. Henry Ford paid for production of a facsimile edition of the 1857 series about the time that he bought William McGuffey's log cabin birthplace and had it moved to his famous Greenfield Village at Dearborn, Michigan.

Criticism of the public school system, especially "Why Johnnie can't read," spawned increasing numbers of private schools. Patrons of these new schools, who often had strong negative feelings about textbooks used in tax-supported institutions, returned to McGuffey's little volumes in droves. New editions of them, handsomely printed but using the language of the University of Virginia faculty member and reproducing their early illustrations, again became best-selling textbooks.

If he could have known that his little books would influence tens of thousands of Space Age boys and girls, the ranking professor at the University of Virginia, widely known as "Old Guff," would have given a quiet smile that signaled, "I told you so!"

After having seen *McGuffey's Readers* through edition after edition, he decided that their style and contents could not be further improved. Always mindful that he came to Charlottesville to teach moral philosophy, Old Guff set to work upon a textbook of philosophy. He spent a decade upon the project, but died before finishing it, quietly conscious, no doubt, that the "moral philosophy" in his little reading books would have far greater impact than the contents of any textbook of philosophy.

24

Booker T. Washington Took His Own Medicine: "Let Your Buckets Down Where You Are"

"Are you the lady that lets boys go to school?"

Miss Mary F. Mackie was startled. Busy reading papers spread on her desk, she had not seen the boy as he stepped timidly into her office. For a moment she made no reply but looked him over critically. *Ragged,* she thought to herself. *And dirty. But eager. Must be about fifteen. Too bad we have no room for him.*

Aloud, she said, "Yes, I let boys go to school . . . when there are places for them. But just now, the institution is full."

Swaying slightly, the young applicant started away. At the door he stopped. Eyes filled with tears but lighted with new hope, he turned back.

"Couldn't I sleep on the floor in the hall?" he begged. "I'm a good hand. Honest, ma'am, I'll work hard. I really will! And I won't eat much. Please let me in! Please!"

Miss Mackie rose. "I believe you mean what you say," she responded as she opened the door of a small classroom next to her office.

"Come here," she directed, pointing to a broom that stood in the corner. "Take this and let me see how well you can clean up this room. While you are working, I will go and talk with General Armstrong about you."

Years later, Booker T. Washington told large audiences about what he termed the most momentous day in his life. "I swept that floor three times," he recalled. "Then I pulled a ragged shirt from my little bundle and dusted every chair in the room four times."

He was standing quietly in a corner when Miss Mackie

Dr. Booker T. Washington, educator, urged both blacks and whites to "Let down your buckets where you are" [TUSKEGEE UNIVERSITY].

returned. Without a word, hardly looking in his direction, she examined the classroom. She moved several chairs and peered into every corner. Then as Washington held his breath, she took a fresh white handkerchief and rubbed it over some of the woodwork.

At last she smiled and said, "I guess we can find a place for you, even if we are already crowded. General Armstrong has consented to let you enter, and you may work as janitor to earn your board and keep. A friend of the general, a gentleman from the North, will pay your tuition."

Born on the plantation of James Burroughs at Hale's Ford in Franklin County, Booker T. Washington is believed to have been the son of a neighboring white man. As a baby, he was listed on plantation records as being worth nothing, but by the time he was about six years old, he was valued at four hundred dollars.

His mother, Jane, gave him the best she had, a few rags for a bed. Just twelve feet wide and sixteen feet long, her shack had no windows. The only floor was the bare earth, and winter rain dripped through the roof.

Slave boys typically received from their owners only one piece of clothing, a tow shirt. Made of flax, such a garment was so coarse and stiff that it tormented its wearer for the first six to eight weeks it was in use. In adult life Booker laughingly told of his brother John, two years his senior, who once did him the great favor of wearing his new shirt for a month to break it in!

Soon after emancipation, Jane and her new husband took their children to Malden, West Virginia, where coal mines and a salt furnace offered hope of jobs. At about age ten, Booker began working fourteen hours a day in the salt mines, earning barely enough to help keep corn bread and sorghum molasses on the family table.

One day he saw a black man reading a newspaper. Never having spent a single day in school, his mind was fired. He, too, would learn to get some sense out of those queer black marks on white paper!

There was not a single piece of printed matter in his mother's cabin, not even a leaf torn from a book; but Booker knew that the barrels with which he worked at the salt mines were marked with names and numbers. By observing them closely, he learned some of the letters of the alphabet. His mother was so impressed that she made great sacrifices to buy a spelling book for him. Studying at night without help, the boy learned to read a few words.

To his joy, a young black opened a school for boys of his own race. Informed of it, Booker's stepfather shook his head. "You gotta work, boy, if you want to eat," he ruled. Weeks later, he relented and agreed to let Booker go to school half-time, provided that he worked in the mines from 4:00 to 9:00 A.M.

On his first day at school, Booker was embarrassed when the teacher asked his full name. Somewhere, he had heard of a great man named Washington, so he responded, "Booker Washington, ma'am." Not until years later did he learn that at birth his mother had named him Booker Taliaferro.

Although Booker did well in school, his stepfather soon brought his studies to an end, making him return to full-time work. Part of the day he toiled in the mines, then worked until night cleaning the house and yard of the owner's wife, Mrs. Lewis Ruffner. Whenever he could, he

Students and faculty members erected many of Tuskegee's buildings [TUSKEGEE UNIVERSITY].

would walk five or six miles to the home of a rural teacher to study a few hours at night, but his progress was slow.

One day the fifteen-year-old overheard two miners talking about a new school for Negro boys at Hampton, Virginia. They said that it was a place where a boy could go without money.

Excited as he had never been before, Booker determined to go to Hampton Institute. He told his brother and his mother about the school. Between them, they got together a few nickels and dimes; and, with his clothing tied in a rag, he set out on the 500-mile trip across the mountains.

He reached Richmond at night, without a cent in his pockets, so he crawled under a plank sidewalk and slept on the ground. Next day, he found work unloading a vessel of pig iron and earned enough money to take a train for the eighty-five remaining miles. When he reached Hampton, he still had fifty cents in his pocket.

After three years he graduated with honor and returned home determined to help less fortunate young blacks. A hastily organized school attracted ninety pupils, yet he found time to teach a class of older students at night and to organize two Sunday schools.

After two years, he spent a term studying at a school in Washington. Then he was called back to Hampton as a teacher. Given a class of seventy-five Indian boys, he was assigned to teach them to speak English. He did so well that Gen. Samuel C. Armstrong, principal of the school, called him to his office one day.

"I have had a letter from 'way down South," he said. "Mr. George W. Campbell, a banker who formerly was a slaveholder, has secured a charter for a Negro normal school that will receive two thousand dollars a year from the state of Alabama. He has asked me to recommend a principal, and I have selected you. I'll find someone to take your place here at Hampton, so I'd like for you to start to Alabama at once."

Upon arrival, Booker T. Washington found that the new school had no building. He managed to get the use of a small church belonging to black worshipers, and in it opened the Tuskegee Normal and Industrial Institute on July 4, 1881. Later, with about two hundred dollars borrowed from a friend back home, he made a down payment on five hundred acres of worn-out farm land and moved to the new site. The buildings of his institute consisted of a stable, a hen house, and the ruins of a partly burned kitchen.

Some of his students wanted to learn Latin and Greek, but Washington told them that it was more important to learn how to make a living. "We need good buildings," he told them, "and good buildings need bricks. Let's all get busy and put up a brick kiln."

When 25,000 handmade bricks were finished, the kiln was constructed. It failed within days, so they tried again. A second failure was followed by a third attempt and a third failure. Washington pawned his watch for fifteen dollars, then made a fourth attempt that proved successful. Students used the kiln to make bricks for the first permanent buildings. Eventually the campus grew to 250 acres and 150 buildings.

Always, Tuskegee's head was busy raising money. He trav-

A national monument to Washington shows him "lifting his veil of ignorance."

eled widely and made many speeches through which he won respect and honor. The slave boy who had fought for a crust of bread had tea with Queen Victoria at Windsor Castle; he became a friend and adviser of President Theodore Roosevelt; Harvard University awarded an honorary degree to the man who first mastered some of his letters by studying salt barrels; and he wrote books that were so well received that they were translated into eighteen languages.

"Let down your buckets where you are," he advised blacks and whites. "When you do that over and over, you will help to bring a new day to the South."

Now Tuskegee University, the institution long headed by Dr. Washington, is a living memorial to him. Elected to the Hall of Fame of Great Americans in 1946, the ex-slave from Franklin County stands for all time as an example of a man who became great despite seemingly insuperable obstacles.

Not simply to the South but to the entire nation, Dr. Booker T. Washington was the prophet of a new era of better racial understanding and more opportunity for blacks. His greatest joy was not reception of another honor, but the thrill of seeing young blacks learn trades, gain educations, and enter mainstream American life.

Index